MEASURING RESEARCH

WHAT EVERYONE NEEDS TO KNOW®

MEASURING
RESEARCH

WHAT EVERYONE NEEDS TO KNOW®

CASSIDY R. SUGIMOTO
AND
VINCENT LARIVIÈRE

OXFORD
UNIVERSITY PRESS

OXFORD
UNIVERSITY PRESS

Oxford University Press is a department of the University of Oxford. It furthers the University's objective of excellence in research, scholarship, and education by publishing worldwide. Oxford is a registered trade mark of Oxford University Press in the UK and certain other countries.

"What Everyone Needs to Know" is a registered trademark of Oxford University Press.

Published in the United States of America by Oxford University Press
198 Madison Avenue, New York, NY 10016, United States of America.

CIP data is on file at the Library of Congress
ISBN 978-0-19-064012-5 (pbk.)
ISBN 978-0-19-064011-8 (hbk.)

1 3 5 7 9 8 6 4 2
Paperback printed by Webcom, Inc., Canada
Hardback printed by Bridgeport National Bindery, Inc., United States of America

This book is dedicated to Noah, Zoé, Anastasia, and Madeleine—who are extraordinary beyond measure.

CONTENTS

3. The Indicators   50

4. The Big Picture   119

MEASURING RESEARCH

WHAT EVERYONE NEEDS TO KNOW®

1

THE BASICS

What is this book about?

Research is a complex social activity. It is performed in a variety of environments by a wide array of actors, and includes many different activities. Production of new knowledge is built upon countless hours of work in laboratories and libraries, meetings with students and collaborators, and formal and informal interactions with other scholars and the public. These activities are difficult, if not impossible, to measure directly. The measurement of research, therefore, is tasked with translating these activities into measurable units—called *indicators*. This book describes the ways in which these indicators are constructed, their strengths and weaknesses, and how they should be interpreted and used.

The measurement of research activity is categorized into three distinct types—input, output, and impact. Input indicators are based on the resources and investments that fuel scientific activities. Common input indicators include the size and other characteristics of the scientific workforce as well as funding allocated to research. Output indicators measure the knowledge that is produced as a result of that input: typically, publications and patents. Impact indicators measure the ways in which scholarly work has an effect upon the research community and society. Identifying and documenting input, output, and impact is difficult, as many traces are not easily visible or fail to manifest themselves entirely. Furthermore, many data traces cannot be easily standardized to allow for measurement at different levels of aggregation. Current measurements of research, therefore, rely on data that leave a trace, can be standardized and aggregated, and are contemporary in nature. This form of research measurement—generally labeled scientometrics—includes all the ways in which we quantitatively gather and analyze data on science—including the production and content of scholarly documents and the traces of the receipt of scholarly products.

Science indicators are constructed from a wide range of data sources. Input data are typically gathered obtrusively by means of local and international surveys. These data have the imprimatur of major governmental and scientific agencies, such as national research councils and international organizations (e.g., the Organisation for Economic Co-operation and Development [OECD] and United Nations Educational, Scientific and Cultural Organization [UNESCO]). The nature of data collection provides an opportunity to gather rich sociodemographic data, and the stability of these organizations leads to routine updates of the data. Output and impact indicators tend to be derived from databases explicitly developed for documentation purposes (e.g., citation indices). The benefits of these unobtrusive data sources are that they provide de facto standards for reporting that are easily aggregated, more comprehensive than local surveys, and relatively stable over time. Despite issues in coverage (e.g., by discipline, language, and country), citation databases have become the standard for measuring research, primarily using the tools of bibliometrics. This book describes these bibliometric data sources as well as newly emerging sources for measuring research.

Research measurement is often seen as promoting a "publish or perish" culture, distorting science, and leading to gross goal displacement. This book examines each of these critiques in turn, highlighting the limitations in data and compilation that need to be considered for appropriate application of indicators. The political economy of research measurement is also of increasing concern, given the few major firms that control data collection (e.g., Clarivate, Elsevier, Google) and the high costs associated with most of these products. This book discusses the notion of science as a public good and the complexities that arise in working with isolated proprietary datasets. Data elitism, lack of access, and interoperability are considered alongside the evolving landscape that is disrupting this historical infrastructure.

Over the last few decades, several advanced handbooks for the compilation and interpretation of bibliometric indicators have been published, mostly by experts from within the community. There is also a comprehensive catalog of technical manuals that provide standards for survey-based measurement of science and technology input indicators. This book is of a different nature: it provides, in accessible terms, an overview of the historical foundations, key concepts and terms, guides to interpretation, critiques, and recommendations for measuring research.

Why measure research?

Science is an object of study across many fields in the humanities and social sciences. Each of these fields brings its own methods to bear on the object of science—from historical, sociological, and philosophical perspectives. Measurements of research—and the indicators that are derived from these measurements—provide unique insights on the relational and contextual elements of science. They can be used both to complement other studies of science as well as to provide additional understanding of how knowledge is produced over time, across disciplines, and across the globe.

Bibliometrics are particularly useful when the amount of data exceeds human capabilities to process. For example, a reviewer is well equipped to make a judgment on a single document or small set of documents. An author can fairly easily ascertain the number of publications he or she produced. However, measurements of the production of an institution or country are harder to gauge. Furthermore, relational data—like citations are nearly impossible to manually analyze even at the level of an individual. Therefore, measurements of research have their greatest utility at scale—to bring into the light that which is not easily observed by the individual.

Curiosity—the fundamental building block of all basic science—fueled much of the early developments in measuring research. Scholars sought to understand the broad and complex system of science using measurements of inputs and outputs. The work of Derek de Solla Price and others used research indicators to construct theories of scientific activity, which were also useful in testing hypotheses posed across different fields of scientific study. For example, philosophers of science have long been interested in consensus and revolutions in science, which can be studied using measurement of research output, topical analysis, and the accumulation of citations. Historians of science have debated the reception of scientific ideas and the impact of specific discoveries on research fields. Analyses of traditional historical documents (archives, interviews, etc.) can be supplemented with bibliometric indicators to demonstrate the receipt by actors at the time of the discovery and subsequently. Sociologists have incorporated research measurement into their analyses to support theories of hierarchies in the structure of science and resulting asymmetries in the distribution of rewards. For all these disciplines, the measurement of research, mostly through scholarly documents, sheds a novel light on science.

Measurement also serves as a mechanism for providing reflective feedback. By turning the tools of science upon science, measurements provide a way to observe and calibrate the system of science. Collection and analysis of information about scientific activity can be used to inform the decisions of administrators and policymakers. Measurements are used to stimulate research, allocate resources, and understand and forecast trends in science. Such measurements can also highlight inequalities in the system. For example, research on gender disparities in science demonstrates the asymmetry between labor and reward in science. The results of these studies can be used to inform policies that aim at improving working conditions and broadening participation in science. This book is about the tools and techniques that make these empirical observations possible and the contextual knowledge needed to make them meaningful.

Who is this book for?

The unparalleled fervor around research evaluation has given rise to a proliferation of tools and available data sources. Historically, research evaluation was done by specialists—primarily scientometricians and dedicated government and university analysts. However, there has been a trend to make data more accessible and place research measurement in the hands of administrators, policymakers, and other scholars. While this is laudable in many respects, it also means that these individuals need to be able to compile and interpret research indicators in a meaningful manner. Many tools attempt to remove the analyst from the raw data, which amplifies the dangers of algorithmic decision-making in research policy. Appropriate use of the tools requires sophisticated knowledge of the data available (and the limitations of these data), an understanding of how indicators are constructed and compiled, and the ability to contextualize the use of these indicators. Indicators are not one-sized nor do they fit all. This book seeks to empower all those who conduct and are subject to research evaluation exercises to be able to meaningfully engage in the measurement of research.

One could argue that, at the most basic level, anyone who can do arithmetic should be able to measure research. While many indicators are constructed with more complicated models, the majority of research indicators are essentially frequency measures and rankings on the basis of these measures. This book, however, provides a description of the complications that can arise in interpreting these data. Some of this complexity comes from a lack of understanding of either the discipline under study or the global context of the scientific system. Scholars, tasked with understanding their own work or the work of others in their domain, can easily address the first of these: In many ways, scholars embedded within a discipline are better suited to understand and address the limitations of the data within their own discipline. Few scholars, however, are trained in a wider understanding of the scientific system, considering issues of disciplinary differences in production and impact.

This book focuses on the peculiarities of bibliometric data: that which makes bibliometric data unique from other types of data. All types of research data—whether from surveys, log files, or archaeological digs—have their own set of limitations. Bibliometric data can provide great insight into the scientific system, but must be understood within its unique context. This requires not only an understanding of the technical and mathematical properties of the data, but also of the larger sociological and economic processes that govern the science system.

Many scientometricians will argue that only experts should evaluate research. There are two problems with this argument. The first is creating an artificial dichotomy between those with bibliometric expertise and "non-experts" when it comes to performing research evaluation. As a matter of practice, the scientific community is self-governing: Peer review is a principal tenet of the system, which rests upon faith in the ability of scholars to evaluate their peers. However, when research evaluation leaves one's domain, many scholars are less equipped to handle the nuances of the data. Expertise is on a spectrum—there is no simple distinction between experts and non-experts in measuring research.

Second, throughout its history, bibliometrics has attracted contributions from scholars coming from a large array of disciplines. While most of the first bibliometricians were natural scientists aiming at understanding the structure of science, the method also attracted scientists interested in providing descriptive accounts of their own disciplines. This led to macro-level analyses as well as iconographic histories of science, focusing on the success of key men and events in science. Sociologists introduced a more theoretical approach, applying social theories to the scientific system. Physicists brought network science and economists brought economic models to the mix. At present, tools are being built to allow individuals to compile their own indicators. As the demand for indicators grows and the users become increasingly diverse, it is necessary to provide a critical and descriptive guide to all those who wish to measure research responsibly. This book is for those individuals.

What are the historical foundations for measuring research?

The origins of research measurement could be traced to several documentation activities—from bibliographic catalogues to labor surveys—extending across time and the globe. However, the historical roots for contemporary research measurement are largely placed in twentieth-century Europe and North America. The early part of the twentieth century saw the development of several fields of research, for example, statistics and sociology, that contributed methods instrumental for research measurement. However, statistical bibliography served as the precursor to most bibliometric methods. This approach, simply the counting of cited documents, was used by librarians to decide what to acquire for their collections. Due to the manual collection of data, these early studies were small scale and driven by specific objectives. Methods were largely built upon the needs of libraries for retrieval and collection management. This origin—and the inextricable relationship between scholarly publishing and libraries—placed bibliometrics, and other quantitative approaches to measuring research, within the domain of library and information science throughout most of the twentieth century.

While the early twentieth century contributed methods that were necessary for measuring research, the mid-twentieth century was characterized by the development of institutions that motivated and facilitated research measurement. The institutionalization of the support of scientific research through research councils changed the political economy of research. As federal institutions began to invest in individual research projects in addition to larger, government-controlled projects, governments increasingly demanded indicators to monitor the progress of scientific research, seen as an essential component of economic growth. Science indicators were a response to this need and a reaction to the renewed sense of international competition for the progress of science. In parallel, the exponential increase in the volume of research necessitated new ways of documenting and retrieving scientific literature. The establishment of the Institute for Scientific Information in the United States, the founding company of the Science Citation Index, was the final piece of institutionalization that enabled the development of science indicators and the rise of a field dedicated to research measurement.

In the early 1960s, Derek de Solla Price—British physicist and historian of science—played a pivotal role in catalyzing a new field around measuring research, drawing inspiration from fellow British physicist John Desmond Bernal, who called for a different approach to the assessment of scholarly production. Previous work in measuring research was nearly always functional in nature—that is, primarily to improve collection management and information retrieval for librarians. Price, however, called for the scholarly community to turn "the tools of science on science itself," noting the intractable relationship between science and society and the importance of studying science with a quantitative lens. Price did not discount the qualitative dimensions, but noted that one must first be "sufficiently scientific in analyzing a whole set of regularities" in science "before beginning to deal humanistically with those irregularities that occur because men are men, and not machines." He called for observation of the general patterns and growth models of science in order to understand more fully the nature of the scientific enterprise. His seminal work, *Little Science, Big Science*, evaluated, inter alia, the volume, velocity, and interaction of scientific information as well as the structural, political, and social properties of science.

One of Price's key observations was that science is essentially contemporary—that is, given the exponential growth rate of science, the majority of scientific outputs have occurred during the present time. This applies to various units of analysis: the number of scientists, number of academic papers, and amount of data. The field of scientometrics, therefore, proved an extremely useful tool in parsing this vast and complex system of science: analyzing the amounts in each category, the relationships among and within variables, and charting the history and predicting the future of science.

The establishment of the Information Science and Scientometric Research Unit at the Library of the Hungarian Academy of Sciences was one of the earliest stand-alone research groups in scientometrics. The launch of the journal *Scientometrics* in 1978, by Hungarian chemist Tibor Braun, further codified the field. It also established the term *scientometrics*—drawn from Russian mathematician and philosopher V. V. Nalimov's term *naukometriya*—as the umbrella term for quantitative studies of science. However, the subtitle to Braun's journal demonstrates the breadth of field envisioned in the 1970s: one that encompassed the science of science, communication in science, and science policy.

Using a literal interpretation of the term, scientometrics is about the construction of metrics of science. Science, of course, is not meant exclusively as the natural sciences, but incorporates all areas of knowledge production (akin to the broader understanding of Latin *Scientia* and German *Wissenschaft*). Although the output of scientometrics is often used for research evaluation purposes, it can also serve as a powerful lens on the scientific system itself. As such, scientometrics is considered a metascience, alongside cousin disciplines such as the history of, philosophy of, and sociology of science—all of which share science as an object of study. In his classic work, Derek de Solla Price wrote of a "prologue to the *science of science*" (italics added). This set out an area of inquiry where scientific and social scientific approaches would be legitimate forms of asking questions about science and measuring research.

Over time, the science of science fractured into two research areas—one called scientometrics and the other science and technology studies—delineated by differing theoretical frameworks (i.e., positivist vs. constructivist approaches) and methods (those typically referred to as quantitative and qualitative). In recent years, a dichotomy between big and small data has also become increasingly divisive. However, the dichotomies between these traditions often promote many false assumptions. Negative interpretations paint quantitative studies as overly reductionist, decontextualized, and therefore artificial. Qualitative studies are seen as nongeneralizable and highly subjective. What opponents of each camp fail to recognize are the fractal distinctions within a field, project, or method, and the ability for both domains to provide insights into the research system at different levels (e.g., micro- vs. macrolevel). Contemporary approaches to the science of science, therefore, should take both approaches into account, triangulating theories and methods. Approaching these domains as complementary, rather than adversarial, provides a more robust lens for understanding science.

What are the theoretical foundations of measuring research?

Initial bibliometric theories were constructed around observed regularities in statistical bibliographies. As early as 1926, Alfred

J. Lotka, a statistician at the MetLife insurance company, found that a minority of researchers were responsible for the majority of documents published. Conversely, a majority of scholars contributed to a minority of documents published. Labeled as Lotka's law, the skewness in researchers' scholarly output has been consistently demonstrated in various datasets and across disciplines—20% of researchers account for 80% of published documents, and 80% of researchers are associated with 20% of published documents. Less than a decade after Lotka's law was proposed, Samuel C. Bradford, a British mathematician and librarian at the London Science Museum, noted that references appeared to follow a similar pattern. He devised Bradford's law of scattering, which observes that the majority of citations are received by relatively few journals, whereas the large majority of journals receive relatively few of the overall citations. The next year, in 1935, American linguist George Kingsley Zipf demonstrated that natural language follows the same type of power law. Zipf's law served as a cornerstone of many early information retrieval systems and has been useful as research measurement has turned toward full-text analysis.

The observation of power laws in research output and impact was instrumental in developing the field. These laws demonstrated that scholarly data diverged from canonical notions of normal distributions, which yield indicative measures of central tendency (i.e., means, medians, modes). By exposing the high skewness of bibliometric data, early theories suggested that bibliometric data operated differently than other types of data. These observations were fundamental for understanding the structure and growth of science. However, developments in research measurement remained largely dormant until the mid-twentieth century, when large-scale citation indices were developed and research assessment became more common.

The rise of research measurement that accompanied the growing availability of data in the 1960s and 1970s was matched by an interest in constructing theories, both scientific and sociological, to explain research output and impact. The sociological companion to statistical theories of skewness came in the form of the Matthew effect, proposed by American sociologist Robert K. Merton in a 1968 paper published in *Science*. Merton investigated how recognition for scientific discoveries is allocated, particularly in the case of simultaneous discoveries. He demonstrated that recognition was more likely to be given to those who already had high degrees of recognition than to those who were less well known. He called this phenomenon the Matthew effect, drawing on the biblical verse that quotes: "For unto every one that hath shall be given, and he shall have abundance: but from him that hath not shall be taken even that which he hath." Following Merton, sociologists (and brothers) Jonathan and Stephen Cole analyzed the social stratification process of science. Using a sample of physicists, they showed that citation-based indicators were related with other indicators of prestige, such as department rankings and awards won. This highlights the disparities of the academic labor system and reinforces Merton's theories of disproportionate allocation of rewards in science.

In 1976, Derek de Solla Price applied these theories to citations and reinforced what he referred to as the "cumulative advantage process" at work in regard to referencing. Several other studies have confirmed the role of cumulative advantage in science: Researchers who are affiliated with prestigious institutions are more likely to receive citations (even when controlling for author and document characteristics), articles in journals of high reputation receive more citations than those in lower regarded journals (controlling again for confounding factors), and researchers who have more citations (as well as publications) are more likely to gain additional citations in a nonlinear manner compared with those who have fewer citations. In short, science, like other social activities, is one where the rich get richer. In parallel, those with little capital also tend to get poorer—a notion examined by historian Margaret

Rossiter and coined as the Matilda effect—referencing the low levels of recognition that women receive for their work.

Theories of cumulative advantage received renewed interest—by a different research community—in the late 1990s, with the introduction of network science as a methodological framework for measuring research. Physicists Albert-László Barabasi and Réka Albert examined what they referred to as preferential attachment in the growth of the World Wide Web. This theory of preferential attachment—an extension of the Matthew effect—has subsequently been used, along with other theories from network science, to study the growth and structure of scientific information.

Capital is a frequently evoked concept in measuring research. Most scholars draw from the theories of capital proposed by French sociologist Pierre Bourdieu. Bourdieu examined the French higher education system (in the wake of the education reform protests of May 1968) and found that forms of power outside of academe were reproduced within the academic system. He looked at these forms of power as types of capital, generated through social, political, and economic means. He proposed academic capital as another form of power in which hierarchies are constructed. Bourdieu argued that those with capital exogenous to science also tended to generate academic capital at a greater rate. Through this process, capital, and, thereby, power, is legitimated and maintained across generations. Bourdieu's theories of capital are critical for understanding exchange of goods in the academic marketplace, which involves the interplay of multiple forms of capital. The academic reward system is held together by the tacit agreement that this capital exists and that measurements provide an indicator of this currency.

In addition to statistics and sociology, scientometricians have also incorporated theories from the semiotic tradition—a discipline that studies how signs and symbols are used for meaningful communication—drawing upon the work of Charles Sanders Peirce, a late nineteenth–early twentieth century American philosopher and logician. Peirce's work focused on the relationship between an object (i.e., signified) and the sign that represents this object. This had obvious implications for measuring science, in which representations of scientific work (i.e., the published document) and scientific impact (i.e., the citation) are used as the basis for indicator construction. Peirce's work was revived by several bibliometricians in the late twentieth and early twenty-first centuries as they grappled with the concept underlying citations. The work of Paul Wouters was particularly relevant in this regard, as he sought to distinguish between the reference, the citation (as represented in a citation index), and the citation as placed in the text.

Henry Small's canonical theory of "cited documents as concept symbols" also derives from the semiotic tradition— although semiotics is never explicitly referenced. Small published his theory on concept symbols in 1978 in *Social Studies of Science*, using British social anthropologist Edmund Leach's definition of a symbol. Small argued that when a reference was placed in a text, it became a symbol for particular ideas, methods, or data. Furthermore, he argued that the scientific community has a high degree of consensus in association between the sign and the concept. He tested the theory by examining the text surrounding references and demonstrated that works are repeatedly evoked for particular types of contributions (e.g., methodological or theoretical). Small's theory of concept symbols has served as the cornerstone for subsequent work on understanding the meaning and motivations underlying citations. This is particularly relevant for indicator construction, wherein the sign and the signified should have high degrees of coherence.

What is an indicator?

In social research—as in the measurement of research—the quantification of concepts is made through the creation of indicators. The strength of the relationship between an indicator and its corresponding concept is critically important for the validity of indicators: An indicator must be explicitly linked to a concept, and there must be sufficient rationale to claim that the indicator represents a valid measurement of that concept. The work of Paul Lazarsfeld, an empirical sociologist, was instrumental in establishing the methodological relationship between concepts and indicators. Lazarsfeld sought to find observable variables that would represent, in a statistically valid manner, unobservable concepts. The measurement of research is derived from this tradition—noting that unobservable variables (such as research production and scientific impact) can be quantified in terms of observable, and, thus, measurable, variables (e.g., number of papers and citations). Indicators, therefore, focus on the observable phenomena of the research enterprise, in a manner that seeks to make manifest the unobservable in research.

The validity of an indicator can be determined by the extent to which it reduces the gap between the measurement and the concept—what historian of science Yves Gingras calls the "adequacy of the indicator for the object it measures." He provides two other key criteria for evaluating indicators, including the "sensitivity to the intrinsic inertia of the object" and the "homogeneity of the dimensions of the indicator." In terms of inertia, Gingras argues that the speed at which an indicator is compiled should match the speed at which the data could be expected to change. The quality of a university, for example, should not witness dynamic changes within a year, making annual rankings inappropriate and annual variations misleading. On the other hand, indicators based on social media data vary much more dynamically; it would therefore be appropriate for these indicators to be constructed and displayed rapidly (if not in real time). Some indicators based on social media violate the third principle, that of homogeneity, in that they incorporate multiple and heterogeneous measures into a single indicator—in addition to, in many cases, not being associated with a clear corresponding concept. For example, the Altmetric Attention Score combines values obtained from Mendeley, Twitter, Facebook, and newspapers (among other sources) into a composite indicator, which makes the indicator uninterpretable.

Indicators can be constructed on the basis of input, output, and impact variables. There are, of course, several questions that require comparison between these types of variables—calculating, for example, the return on research investment. However, such indicators are complicated by the lack of globally comparable input indicators as well as the skewness in coverage in citation indices. Imagine, for example, if one wanted to compare whether investment in research in China led to higher returns (of research output) than investment in research in the United States. This would make several assumptions: (a) that investment is calculated in the same way for both China and the United States, (b) that coverage of research output was equal for both countries (or that inequalities were calculated into the measurement), (c) that both measurements were appropriately normalized for size of the scientific work (which must be calculated equally), and (d) that output was normalized by the disciplinary emphasis of the countries. These calculations are not impossible, but much more complicated than those produced by simply taking one reported R&D variable and dividing it by the number of publications from that country. It is critical, therefore, that those constructing and interpreting indicators have a strong understanding of the strengths and weaknesses of various databases as well as an accurate understanding of how science indicators are constructed.

What are the data sources for measuring research?

Data sources used to measure research can be divided into two broad categories: those used for input indicators and those used for output and impact indicators. Data collection of input variables is often performed at the local level through research councils or through large-scale surveys, by several organizations that have sought to aggregate these local collection activities. For example, the OECD and UNESCO have worked since the early 1960s to create standards for the conceptualization and operationalization of data on research activity. The OECD, through the National Experts on Science and Technology Indicators working group, has created several manuals (colloquially known as the Frascati, Canberra, and Oslo manuals) that provide basic definitions and guidelines for the compilation of research and development (R&D) indicators. The Frascati manual, arguably the dominant manual, provides definitions for key concepts, such as "basic research," "applied research," and "experimental development," as well as disciplinary taxonomies. These lengthy and detailed definitions are crucial, because they determine what type of activities (and associated expenditures and human resources) should and should not be counted.

These manuals on input indicators are revised periodically to ensure that indicators are following the changes in the social practices they aim at measuring. However, each country has idiosyncratic practices on how they both collect and report input variables, making global comparisons difficult. Data are aggregated in reports, with a healthy dose of footnotes to highlight the specificities of data collection in each country and inconsistencies in the data. For example, footnotes include statements such as "Do not correspond exactly to OECD norms," "Break in series with previous year for which data is available," or "Overestimated or based on overestimated data." While these manuals provide the best available source of input indicators, their inability to create systematic and globally comparable indicators remains a concern. In parallel with macrolevel datasets generally compiled at the level of countries, increasingly, states/provinces, industrial sectors, and research councils—such as the National Science Foundation and National Institutes of Health in the United

States—are making data on funded projects available in online systems. However, these datasets are mostly available for individual funders or in systems that cover funders from a specific country or for specific fields, which complicates international or multidisciplinary comparisons. Although there are a few initiatives to merge some of these datasets and create tools that cover several funders, these remain far from comprehensive.

Input indicators collected by local and interstate organizations tend to focus on disciplines suited to R&D assessments, that is, science, technology, engineering, and medicine (STEM). The analysis of the arts and humanities, as well as some social sciences, are traditionally removed from reports from the OECD and other large national reports (such as the NSF Science and Engineering Indicators in the United States). Therefore, when deriving the state of research for a given country, input indicators should be interpreted as the strength of the natural, physical, and medical sciences in that country. There are also coverage issues at the level of country: While countries with strong investments in science tend to invest in evaluations of their input variables, the same is not true for scientifically poorer countries, leading to a lack of globally comprehensive input indicators.

Bibliographic databases that have been developed for research documentation purposes have served as the dominant source of data on outputs and impact, and have provided a standard that is systematically updated. There are several indices of published literature that are useful for deriving output indicators on research production, collaboration, and impact. Some of these, such as MEDLINE, provide global coverage of specific domains, while others, such as SciELO in Brazil, focus on national journals. However, there are relatively few sources providing comprehensive citation data. Among these, the three most well known include the Web of Science, Scopus, and Google Scholar. These are distinguished from publication databases—such as MEDLINE—in that they provide relational information in the form of citation connections in addition to publication metadata. In other words, they provide, for each citing paper, a list of cited references. Another important characteristic of the Web of Science and Scopus is that they include authors' addresses, which allows for the assignation of papers to institutions and countries.

Each of these sources is a product of their time: the Science Citation Index—now part of the multidisciplinary Web of Science database—was the first comprehensive citation index, influenced by legal databases, modeled for librarians and information scientists, and constructed in a predigital era. This context is evident in both the strengths and weaknesses of the index. Scopus, on the other hand was built in the digital era and was able to improve upon the weaknesses of Web of Science. It also builds upon a large corpus of journals and with the vast management and backing of the world's largest publisher of scholarly journals (Elsevier), it was able to challenge the monopoly of the Web of Science. Google Scholar was also created within an existing corporation, and relied on Google's massive indexation capabilities rather than on precise curation of content. These contextual elements are necessary to understand the strengths and weaknesses of these sources.

Disciplinary oriented datasets can also be used for the measurement of research. For instance, MEDLINE—hosted and curated by the US National Library of Medicine—covers almost all medical papers and is freely available (and can be downloaded and processed with relatively little technical sophistication). It provides coverage since the 1950s and has one of the most precise and well-curated topical categorization systems among research datasets: MeSH headings. MeSH headings provide a hierarchically organized terminology that contains detailed information on papers indexed, from diseases to methods used and populations analyzed, making it an ideal data source for those wanting to study the topical landscape of the medical domain. The main issue with MEDLINE from a bibliometric perspective is that it does not include cited references and, until recently, only the first (or main) institutional address of a paper was listed; therefore, it can measure research production—with limitations—but not scholarly impact. Furthermore, given that it was created for retrieving rather than counting papers, it has less metadata. For example, institutional addresses for all authors were only provided since 2015 (before this, only the institution of the first author was provided). Therefore, it is impossible to create collaboration measures or institutional production measures that occurred before this time. Merging MEDLINE with other citation indices (e.g., Web of Science or Scopus) combines the advantages of MEDLINE (such as MeSH) with the relational capabilities and metadata of a citation index.

There are relatively few comprehensive sources for the measurement of research produced in books. WorldCat—a network of library content and services—is arguably the most comprehensive source for measuring the production of books. This source provides an indication, globally, of the holdings of libraries. Output indicators can be calculated according to the number of libraries holding particular items, by year and disciplinary category. However, this tool has been underutilized in bibliometric research, largely because although it provides an indication of production, it does not provide citation linkages. The Book Citation Index, produced by Thomson Reuters, was the first book citation index. However, this source repeats many of the coverage flaws from the original Web of Science; that is, it is biased toward US books, from major publishers, in STEM, and written in English. A more comprehensive database is provided by Google Books. This source, however, lacks the transparency necessary for systematic research evaluation: There is no indication of the method for retrieval and, as a result, no clear indication of the population or sample. Moreover, as with any Google product, it is relatively difficult—if not impossible—to collect the raw data it contains.

Other data sources and tools have emerged in recent years to challenge the monopoly of citation indices over the measurement of research production and impact. These include data sources that trace the impact of research on the social web and mentions of articles outside the scientific literature, for example, in policy documents, on social media, and in the mainstream media. These have broadened the sources of attention for scholarship. In addition, there is a growing interest in providing traces of attention not just of journal articles—the dominant genre in traditional citation indices—but also of books, data, and other forms of scholarship. For example, OCLC, the company that owns WorldCat, entered into a partnership in 2013 to integrate WorldCat data into Plum Analytics, a company that aggregates altmetric data for libraries and institutions. The company Altmetric also provides indicators for books of specific publishers. However, these sources remain on the periphery for research evaluation exercises. Patents and journal articles, therefore, have served as nearly exclusive data sources for the measurement of research output.

2
THE DATA

What is a citation index?

A citation index is a bibliographic database that contains, in addition to basic metadata on information resources—such as authors, publication year, title of documents, and journal names—the references made by these documents, which allows for the creation of citation links between documents. The model for the first science citation index was imported from the legal field, which had long employed Shepard's Citations, a legal citatory developed in 1873 in the United States by Frank Shepard. This legal citation index provided, for law, an embedded network of cases in which one could examine provenance and precedence. Chemist and information scientist Eugene Garfield saw in this a model for the scientific literature and revealed, in a 1955 *Science* publication, a proposal for a science citation index. The subtitle of his article, "A new dimension in documentation through association of ideas," demonstrates that his underlying goal was not to evaluate research (as is often assumed), but rather to link articles by their conceptual similarities. He described his proposed index as an "association-of-ideas index" because it would allow people to traverse across journals and disciplines by means of "ideas," which Garfield argued was the "molecular unit" of scientific work. Garfield proposed that such an index would be useful for retrieval, but also to curtail inappropriate citation behavior, by bringing to light "uncritical" citations and making visible all the antecedents of a work. Scholars would then be able to identify relevant work, on the underlying assumption that those works cited by and citing a relevant work were also likely to be relevant.

Garfield's proposal for a citation index received support from individuals such as Nobel Laureate and geneticist Joshua Lederberg, who championed the project; and the National Institutes of Health and the National Science Foundation, which provided initial funding. Garfield piloted a genetics citation index in the late 1950s, using punch cards and magnetic tapes. This served as the prototype and proof-of-concept for the Science Citation Index (SCI), which was further developed by Garfield's company, the Institute for Scientific Information, founded in 1960. In 1963, Garfield published the first SCI, which contained 613 journals covering all disciplines and was available to scholars and libraries in paper format. The primary intention was retrieval, rather than the measurement of research, and the SCI was novel in that it allowed researchers not only to search by journal or by the names of authors, but also to identify relationships based on the references shared among documents. A document thereby became embedded in a network of relationships, and this network could be traversed to follow an idea or concept across disciplinary boundaries. The interdisciplinary nature of this type of information retrieval was unique and size dependent: In order to be used to its full potential, a citation index needs to cover a relatively large and interdisciplinary corpus. A citation index based solely on a few journals would only contain a small proportion of references to other documents and would be ineffective as a retrieval tool. Therefore, one key attribute of a citation index is the number of citing documents, called *source items*.

In addition to these citing–cited relationships, citation indices also contain additional geographic information, which is critical for constructing indicators at the meso- and macro-levels. For example, a good citation index will provide full institutional addresses of all authors, including department, institution, city, province/state, and country. Of course, the availability of these data is dependent upon what is provided by scholarly journals: many journals in the arts and humanities, for example, do not provide authors' addresses, leading to a lower coverage of these variables. There are also disciplinary differences in the reporting of other metadata. For example, in many subfields of physics and mathematics, initials are provided rather than full given names, which limits author disambiguation—that is, being able to identify which distinct author is associated with which publications, across the entire dataset—and individual-level analyses. Citation indices are also beginning to incorporate the acknowledgment section of papers, but including only those that contain funding information. This inevitably leads to an overrepresentation of acknowledgments from highly funded domains (e.g., natural and medical sciences). In addition to these variables explicitly indexed, other layers of information can be added by analysts and overlay tools. For example, authors can be assigned to genders, institutions can be assigned to sectors, and papers can be assigned to topics.

Topic information has typically been derived from metadata such as the title, abstract, and keywords. However, as contemporary documents are born digital and older documents are being digitized, a new opportunity is available for the analysis of the full text of articles. Much of this full-text content is proprietary (e.g., JSTOR), though the expansion of preprint and postprint repositories is making more data available. Of course, there are also several attempts at constructing full-text repositories through pirating (e.g., Sci-Hub), though these remain used for reading, rather than the measurement of research. Overall, the analysis of full text for science indicators remains at an early stage. Tools such as Semantic Scholar are beginning to make use of full-text and advances in machine learning to provide more precise retrieval. Semantic Scholar has suggested several indicators on the basis of full-text analysis, including highly influential citations based on the context surrounding each citation. However, the data indexed are limited to two domains (computer science and neuroscience) and publications in English. Furthermore, the source only provides limited data for articles behind a paywall. Yet, this initiative provides an example of some of the opportunities for measuring research with full-text data. Full-text will likely be an area of future development for citation indices and research measurement.

What is the Web of Science?

The Web of Science (WoS)—also known as the Web of Knowledge—is the modern version of the SCI, developed by Eugene Garfield and first released in 1963. The WoS platform is currently commercialized by Clarivate Analytics—owned by Onex Corporation and Barlng Private Equity Asia, who purchased it from Thomson Reuters in 2016 for 3.55B USD. As the first citation index for research, the SCI focused exclusively on the natural and medical sciences. In 1973, the Social Science Citation Index (SSCI) was created, and in 1975, an index was added for the Arts and Humanities (AHCI). The order of expansion, coupled with the differences in volume of production of journal articles across domains—versus other document types, such as books and conference proceedings—has led to skewness in terms of disciplinary coverage within the WoS. Specifically, the coverage of the natural and medical sciences is higher than the social sciences—and the coverage is lowest in the arts and humanities.

Creator Garfield never sought for the SCI to be an exhaustive database; rather, he aimed to curate a selective list of journals that were the most important for their respective disciplines. He used Bradford's law of scattering as the core principle. This law dictates that the majority of cited literature in a domain is concentrated in a few journals and, conversely, that the majority of scholarly journals contain a minority of cited documents. In other words, Bradford's law suggests that references made to journals follows a Pareto distribution, in which there is a minority of journals at the core and a majority of journals at the periphery. Garfield's goal was to index these core journals, based on the number of citations they received. This approach worked fairly well in the natural and medical sciences, but required supplemental selection criteria for the arts and humanities, due to the low coverage of source items. A journal can also request indexation. Garfield was transparent about the limitations of coverage and the pressures that he felt in making selections, including financial concerns. He repeatedly emphasized that he was running a business, not a nonprofit organization, particularly when he was criticized for allowing journals to pay for inclusion, provided they met the quality criteria.

Likely as a result of the higher coverage of Scopus, WoS has clarified its indexing policy in a recent essay published on its website, emphasizing the importance of being "selective." Criteria currently used include publishing standards (e.g., peer review, regularity in publishing, and the use of English), editorial content, international scope of the journal, as well as citation-based criteria. These various factors are analyzed jointly by internal staff, who ultimately decide on the inclusion or exclusion of the journal. The WoS indexing policy also mentions the importance of taking local and regional topics into account for inclusion in the SSCI and AHCI; however, how these are incorporated remains relatively imprecise. The WoS was initially built as a retrieval tool and oriented toward librarians and other expert searchers. Due to this, metadata was included that made possible certain types of retrieval; for example, very early in the history of the SCI—in 1973—the database included institutional affiliation of authors, likely to allow a scholar or librarian to perform a search to identify articles from a particular institution, city, or country. Furthermore, the WoS indexed the institutional addresses of all authors, not just first authors as is done in other databases (e.g., MEDLINE). This facilitated the construction of collaboration indicators, as one could quickly identify, at scale, collaboration patterns between affiliations at multiple levels of aggregation (e.g., institutions, cities, countries). The limitation was that, although all the institutional addresses were provided, they were not linked with individual authors until 2008, making author disambiguation difficult to perform automatically, as the precise affiliation of each author was unknown in cases of interinstitutional collaboration. Furthermore, it was not until 2008 that given names of authors were provided. This means that, prior to 2008, a search for J. Smith aiming at retrieving papers by John Smith would retrieve papers from Jonathan Smith, Jim Smith, etc. Furthermore, contrary to Scopus—which includes an author disambiguation algorithm—WoS does not automatically disambiguate but relies instead on a ResearcherID, which requires manual curation by authors and has not seen widespread adoption. As a result, while the WoS is useful for analyses at aggregate levels (e.g., subject, journal, institution, city, state/province, country), individual-level bibliometrics remain a challenge when this data source is used.

Other criticisms have also been leveled at the SCI and successors. Bias in coverage is always the most critical, with critics noting the disparities in terms of journals, fields, genre, geography, and language of what is indexed. In addition, there is concern over differential levels of quality of indexing, with non-English-language material having a much higher degree of indexing errors (which makes both retrieval and disambiguation more difficult). Of critical concern is the quality of the indexation of references, which can lead to an underestimation of the citations received by papers and journals. However, as Garfield was quick to point out from the beginning, the quality of the index is dependent upon the quality of the underlying material, and the index cannot correct for error on the part of authors, editors, or publishers. Due to the reliance on content from publishers, there is also the concern of the delayed registration of citations, an obstacle that is overcome with sources such as Google Scholar.

Another key issue is the coverage of references made by the indexed papers, which, taken globally, provides an indication on the applicability of citation analysis to specific domains. For example, if one considers the percentage of source items within the reference list—that is, the percentage of items cited by indexed papers that are also in the WoS—it is clear that although the WoS is fairly comprehensive in its indexation of the published literature in the natural and medical sciences, it provides fairly low coverage of source items in the social sciences, arts, and humanities. While about 85% of all material cited by 2015 papers in the medical sciences goes to other documents indexed in the database, this percentage is lower in the natural sciences (below 75%) and in the social sciences (just above 50%) (Figure 2.1). In the arts and humanities only a small fraction of references by WoS documents link to other documents in the database (about 10%). Trends are increasing in all domains, which suggests that the WoS coverage of relevant literature is improving (or that WoS-indexed journals

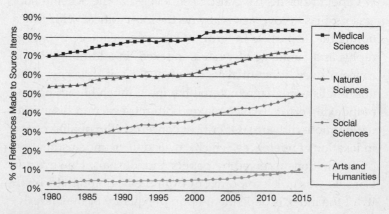

Figure 2.1 Percentage of references made to source items (i.e., other documents that are indexed in the Web of Science), 1980–2015.

Source: Web of Science, aggregated NSF disciplines.

are increasingly self-referencing). This may also be an effect of a change in researchers' publication and citation behavior, which might increasingly rely on journal articles rather than books and other types of documents.

The advent of the CD-ROM in the first half of the 1990s facilitated the use of the index for large-scale research evaluation and fueled the creation of specialized bibliometric research units and third-party analysis. Furthermore, the construction of INCITES—an analytical layer on top of the raw citation data that provides bibliometric indicators and benchmarking analyses—expanded the pool of potential users. The market value of this has since been realized by other corporations, such as Academic Analytics, who market indicator and benchmarking data to institutions and, to a lesser extent, individuals.

In order to expand the breadth and coverage of the data that they provide, Thomson Reuters created the Conference Proceedings citation Index in 1990 and the Book Citation Index in 2008. The former focused on expanding the reach of the products in fields such as engineering and computer science, whereas the Book Citation Index sought to address the limitations in coverage across the social sciences. In 2012, in response to the growing emphasis on open data, Thomson Reuters created the Data Citation Index. The index is dominated by clinical medicine: In 2013, four repositories accounted for 75% of all records—Gene Expression Omnibus, UniProt Knowledgebase, PANGAEA, and the US Census Bureau TIGER/Line Shapefiles. In addition to these main citation indices, Clarivate (the successor to Thomson Reuters) also indexes several regional indices, including the SciELO Citation Index, the Russian Science Citation Index, the Chinese Science Citation Database, and the KCI Korean Journal Database, which increases the coverage of the database by a few million records. However, the interoperability of these indices with the main platform, as well as their availability, is not perfect, which has led to very little use.

On the whole, the entire WoS suite covers, as of December 2016, papers published in about 12,700 journals, 160,000 conference proceedings, and 68,000 books, for a total of approximately 55 million documents and 1.1 billion reference links going back to 1900. Although all records indexed in the WoS include cited references, the WoS can be considered "comprehensive"—that is, covering all disciplines and consistent in its indexing practices—from 1980 onwards.

What is Scopus?

The monopoly of the WoS over large-scale bibliometric analysis ended in 2004, when the world's largest scholarly publisher, Elsevier, released the Scopus citation index. Prior to the creation of Scopus, researchers would search for scholarly papers using other databases (e.g., WoS), obtain bibliographic information, and then retrieve them on Elsevier's Science Direct. The establishment of Scopus is often heralded as a successful case of vertical integration, in which the firm that creates the citation index also owns the material it is indexing. This is a fundamental difference from the WoS, which relies on publishers to deposit material in order to extract the necessary metadata. Elsevier, on the other hand, already owns the material and has metadata readily available. Thus, Elsevier seized the opportunity to create a citation index constructed from the backbone of journals owned by the company, although Elsevier chose not to index the entire catalog—possibly to alleviate concerns that the index was not selective enough. As of 2016, about 10% of journals indexed in the Scopus database are Elsevier titles. Vertical integration, while a benefit for the company, has led to some concerns about monopolies in scholarly communication given that Elsevier now serves as a major indexer, publisher, and provider of research evaluation tools.

Given its more restrictive access and data purchase policies for third-party reuse of data, full analysis of Scopus's coverage and limitations is more difficult to provide. Whereas the WoS has always claimed to be relying on citation data, Scopus was initially more elusive in the criteria for inclusion. A Content Selection and Advisory Board was eventually created, including both scientists and librarians, which evaluates journals for inclusion. In addition to basic criteria (e.g., peer-reviewed, presence of ISSN), the content selection board assesses journals according to five criteria: editorial policy, content, citedness, regularity in publishing, and online availability. Indexed journals are also subject to periodical reevaluation, and might be flagged because of high self-citation rates or a low overall number of papers, citations, and full-text clicks. Elsevier has not published, however, how many journals have been removed from the platform since its creation.

The indexation of books is less clear. While criteria include reputation of the publisher, quality of books, or publication policies, the operationalization of these concepts is not provided. Indexation is based on the publisher, rather than on individual book titles. Similarly, the indexing of conference proceedings is based on the quality of the conference, as well as on the reputation of the organization or publisher behind it. On the whole, the selection criteria seem to have resulted in a more inclusive database, in terms of document types, total titles, and coverage of national journals—all of which were concerns that the research and the bibliometric communities had with WoS. Another important feature of Scopus is the built-in author disambiguation, which automatically assigns papers to individual researchers with a high level of precision—although the methodology behind the algorithm has not been disclosed.

The first release of Scopus excluded Arts and Humanities, knowing that these domains were not well covered by journal literature, and that applicability of citation analysis suffered from several limitations. As of 2016, Scopus indexed more than 60 million records across all disciplines, coming from about 23,000 journal titles, as well as 6 million conference proceeding papers, and 130,000 books. However, Scopus is a much younger database in terms of coverage—it contains records going back to 1823, but is only consistent in indexing from 1996 onwards. This makes it a high-quality source for contemporary analyses, but of inferior quality to WoS for historical analyses.

What is Google Scholar Citations?

One year after Scopus, in 2005, Google Scholar came onto the scene as a tool for researchers to find and retrieve the full text of documents. A few years after the introduction of the tool, bibliometric indicators were added to the online platform at the individual and journal level—although the latter is quite limited—under the rubric Google Scholar Citations. The algorithm underlying the content of Google Scholar Citations is not well publicized: There are no details on methods nor explanation of the search algorithm other than a brief note on coverage available on the website, which emphasizes, among other things, that Google Scholar covers papers (or documents), rather than journals. It is assumed that Google Scholar retrieves all papers that are in institutional or disciplinary repositories, placed on scholars' websites, and on scholarly journal websites. It also indexes works across multiple languages; for example, Google Scholar began indexing Russian-language articles in 2016. However, Google Scholar often aggregates nonjournal articles—from PowerPoint presentations to book chapters, basically anything that bears the trappings of an academic document. Although there is no precise way to measure the total number of documents, it has been estimated at about 160 million documents, which would make it the largest citation index.

Given the heterogeneity of the sources and their automatic indexation, Google Scholar's data is incomplete and of relatively poor quality. Institutional affiliations, contrary to WoS and Scopus, are not available through the platform. Rather, the bibliometric aspect of Google Scholar Citations is limited to individual and journal-level metrics, as these are the only indicators it aggregates. The platform provides total citations, h-index, and i10-index (the number of papers that have at least 10 citations). Any scholar can create a profile, and Google Scholar Citations will automatically attribute documents to each author. This retrieval process is done dynamically, which means that a scholar's record may increase and decrease on any given day, based on the availability of data sources. The instability of the record complicates the use of this data source for measuring research, making comparisons, diachronic analyses, and replicability difficult. Each author has the ability to curate his or her own list—merging duplicate records and deleting inaccurate records. However, there is relatively little incentive to do this, as merging and deleting both reduce the productivity and impact scores associated with the scholar's record. Therefore, although the dynamicity of Google Scholar Citations makes it highly appealing in that it provides the most up-to-date citation statistics, it is problematic for research evaluation because production and citation rates can change daily in either direction (with decreasing numbers from deleting inappropriately attributed sources and merging duplicates).

Furthermore, Google Scholar has a high amount of duplication and of inclusion of nonscientific documents as well as incorrectly attributed works of scholarship, due to the use of automatic indexing and author disambiguation techniques. For example, Google Scholar Citations profiles often include articles not authored by the author (or a homonym) and entries listed multiple times with different name variants. This is highly problematic, as it grossly inflates both productivity and impact measures. The validity of the data indexed by— and thus results compiled with—Google Scholar have been tested in a few empirical studies. For instance, Cyril Labbé, a French computer scientist, created in 2009 a set of 101 automatically generated papers that all cited each other—as well as a reference to a paper already in Google Scholar, in order to ensure indexing by the platform—which led to Ike Antkare (a fictional researcher) holding the record as one of the most cited researchers of all time, with an h-index around 100. Similarly, a group of Spanish researchers from the EC3 Research Group in Granada provided a demonstration on how easy it is to inflate one's own citation rates. While Labbé used SciGen to generate false documents, these scholars simply pasted the same short text repeatedly in a paper-style document, which only cited documents from their own research group. They also created a false researcher—named Marco Alberto Pantani-Contador (with reference to two doping cyclists)—who authored six documents that cited the research group's paper 129 times, increasing their citation rates by 774 citations. What is even more interesting is Google's inability to detect the hoax: It was only after the authors went public—through the publication of a working paper and a blog post—that Google Scholar deleted the Pantani-Contador profile. Both hoaxes speak to the fundamental issue with Google Scholar: its inability to distinguish genuine research papers from documents that only "look" like scholarly documents.

While the coverage of Google Scholar is much broader than that of the other two citation indices—which makes coverage obtained closer to, and sometimes greater than, researchers' CVs—it does not contain all of the capabilities of the other two citation indices. For instance, one cannot retrieve or download records, and there is no population size or baseline given for comparison, as there is with the WoS and Scopus. A secondary tool, however, was developed in 2006 to provide advanced bibliometric indicators for sets of papers indexed by Google Scholar. Anne Wil-Harzing—who at the time was a faculty member at the University of Melbourne, Australia—developed the tool Publish or Perish (PoP), which is a software program that analyzes Google Scholar data and constructs various metrics on these data. The software is limited to 1,000 records, which defaults to the highest retrieved items unless otherwise specified. The tool allows for the construction of more meaningful indicators than with Google Scholar alone. However, neither more advanced bibliometric indicators nor global, institutional, or disciplinary analyses are possible with the tool due to the size limitations as well as its dependence on the opacity of Google Scholar data and algorithm. Furthermore, the quality of the metadata through PoP is quite limited, as some author names are not provided, journal names are not standardized, and institutional information is not available. In short, this tool provides a rough estimate of productivity and impact for an individual or small research team, but provides little else in terms of measuring research systematically.

What are the differences among the main citation indices?

The three main citation indices vary in both size and coverage. Google Scholar was estimated at about 160 million documents in 2014, compared with 60 million in Scopus and 55 million in the WoS. However, Google Scholar lacks historical depth, as it strictly indexes papers available online. High-quality data in Scopus is also limited to contemporary records, as they only index authors and affiliations from 1996 onward. The WoS has the most historical depth, providing indexing from 1900 to the present, although data from the early twentieth century are relatively sparse.

In terms of titles, nearly all of the source items from the WoS can also be found in Scopus. More specifically, Scopus has a broader coverage of the social sciences and arts and humanities than the WoS—whose coverage of those disciplines has remained stable or even decreased over time. Scopus has made more of a commitment to indexing the arts and humanities— despite excluding them in its first release—particularly through inclusion of national journals, which are of central importance in many social sciences and humanities disciplines. The only disciplines in which WoS coverage exceeds Scopus are the natural sciences—possibly due to the original focus in these areas. It is impossible to compare exact title coverage between Google Scholar and the other indices. However, due to the exclusive focus on online papers, Google Scholar's coverage of the arts and humanities is likely more limited, given that a sizeable proportion of these journals are still only available in print and open access in these fields remains low.

Qualities of data standardization vary across the databases. The WoS has a reputation for higher data quality, due to long-established practices developed across five decades of work. Initial indexing practices were developed in a predigital era, which prized highly curated and standardized fields in order to minimize disk space. Early indexing in the WoS was also done from the print versions of documents, which allowed for indexing of multiple aspects of the document, including manual indexing of document types and standardized abbreviations for institutional addresses. Scopus data lacked this high level of indexing initially, given that it relied heavily on metadata inputted for a different purpose (i.e., publishing rather than retrieval). Although data quality has improved, it remains below that of WoS, especially in terms of institutional addresses of authors. Google Scholar has the poorest quality data of the three, as no manual cleaning or indexing is performed and it relies exclusively on automatic indexing.

In terms of author disambiguation, Scopus is more accurate. The early citation indices of Thomson Reuters did not create a unique identifier for authors and did not begin indexing first names until 2008. Google Scholar performs an initial assignment of documents to authors, which requires manual curation by the individual author. This leads to high variability in the reliability of the disambiguation: A scholar must have both constructed and cleaned their own profile in order for the data to be accurate. This may seem a trivial and technical point; however, it is critical for individual-level bibliometrics: Without clear author disambiguation, measuring research at the level of an individual is highly fraught with error and severe implications for the ranking of scholars.

Another issue is that of document types: While both WoS and Scopus categorize scholarly documents as research articles, review articles, editorials, letters to the editor, etc., Google

Scholar does not perform such categorization, which makes it impossible to restrict analyses to peer-reviewed documents. Although the WoS and Scopus do not use the exact same document categorization, they generally agree on what represents research and review articles, which are typically considered as original, peer-reviewed contributions to knowledge.

Despite these concerns in data standardization, there is a clear differentiation in terms of use. Figure 2.2 presents the Google search data for each of the three citation indices since 2004. This is, of course, only an indication of those individuals who have searched for these databases within Google—many users of the WoS and Scopus are likely searching for these databases within the walls of a library search engine. Yet, it is clear that Google Scholar is growing in popularity at a rate

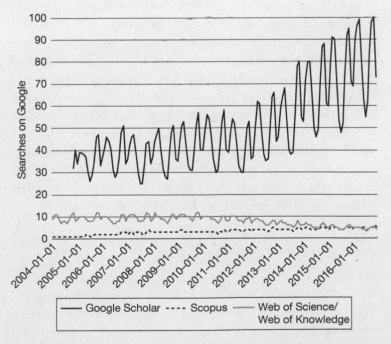

Figure 2.2 Google searches (max = 100) for the three main citation indices, 2004–2016. Source: Google Trends.

unmatched by Scopus and WoS. While the ratio between the WoS, Scopus, and Google Scholar remained relatively stable until late 2011, the release of a new version of Google Scholar in which academics could create their own citation profiles led to a strong increase in interest, as well as a slow relative decrease in interest in WoS, whose second position was overtaken by Scopus in 2015. This demonstrates a potential difference in use for retrieval, not for research measurement, but is indicative of the growing market share for Google Scholar and, to a lesser extent, Scopus.

In summary, there are several things to consider in the use of a specific data source (beyond access to the data source itself): the balance between exhaustivity and access, the quality of necessary data, and the type of measurement that one needs to conduct. For example, Google Scholar is not well suited for collaboration or institutional indicators and can only be used (with caution) for individual-level bibliometrics. Scopus cannot be used for historical analyses, and the WoS does not perform well for individual-level bibliometrics without additional disambiguation. One must also take into account genre and disciplinary concerns: scholars in the social sciences and arts and humanities are better covered in Scopus than in WoS, while for the natural and medical sciences, both databases yield relatively similar results. Convenience is often the justification for selection of an index, but researchers should acknowledge the inherent limitations in each of these databases and consider whether the data are fit for the purpose for which they are intended.

What are the cultural biases of data sources?

Data sources for research indicators are not value neutral. Rather, they are the products of historical, political, economic, and social contexts. This is perhaps most apparent in the large biases in coverage by language and geography. Although it is acknowledged that the WoS does not represent the population of all published research, many still hold the misconception that it represents a generalizable sample. Unfortunately, unlike a quota or stratified sample, there is significant unevenness by country of author. Articles written by authors from the United States comprise nearly a quarter of all authorships in both the WoS and Scopus. China, the United Kingdom, Germany, and Japan (in that order) are the next most productive countries in both databases. India is the sixth most productive in Scopus, whereas France is ranked sixth in the WoS. This is an artifact of the different sources indexed by the two databases, with the WoS having greater coverage from Western countries, whereas Scopus has higher coverage from non-Western countries.

Yet, a simple comparison between sources does not reveal the relationship between coverage and the true production of scholarship in the world. Ulrich's Periodical database provides a closer approximation of this in that it attempts an exhaustive indexing of all periodicals in the world, with corresponding metadata. Although it does not provide information on the volume of production or the authors within the journals, it provides a sense of the title coverage by the various databases. Studies have demonstrated that the Netherlands, the United Kingdom, and the United States are overrepresented in every field—that is, that journals from these countries are disproportionately indexed in the major citation indices. This is likely due to the concentration of publishers in these countries. There are, however, differences by discipline. For example, in the social sciences, Australia and Germany are overrepresented in the WoS, yet underrepresented in Scopus. WoS has higher representation of French journals in the arts and humanities, whereas Scopus has a much greater coverage of Chinese, Indian, and Russian arts and humanities journals.

Parallels can be seen in an examination of the language in which research is written. The language of scholarship has changed dramatically across the twentieth century. At the beginning of the 20th century, German, English, and French shared nearly equal market shares of published research. This changed after the Second World War, with English and Russian emerging as the two main publication languages, particularly in the natural and medical sciences. The end of the Soviet Union led to a marked decline of the use of Russian, leaving English as the common language of science. Thus, while both WoS and Scopus are considered to have an English-language bias, so does science.

English represents nearly 95% of all indexed papers in the WoS and 87% of those indexed in Scopus (Figure 2.3). This trend is observed for all four broad domains. This larger coverage of non-English literature is mostly a consequence of a broader coverage by Scopus, as both databases share the same core of English-language periodicals. The databases also share the same most frequent languages—Chinese, English, French, German, Japanese, Russian, and Spanish—though the dominance of these varies by database and discipline. Scopus has a larger proportion of Chinese papers (4.2% vs. 0.3%) than the WoS. Russian papers have greater coverage in the WoS than Scopus, which is likely a reflection of the larger historical coverage. French and German are covered to a similar extent by both databases, though the WoS has a larger proportion of papers in these two languages in the arts and humanities. Languages other than the top seven account for 3% of Scopus, but less than 1% of the WoS.

These trends have not been stable over time (Figure 2.4). Over the last 35 years, there has been a clear anglicization of the WoS database—except in the arts and humanities—which is likely a reflection of the anglicization of research in general. For instance, while English accounted for 83% to 85% of medical and natural sciences papers in 1980, this percentage rose to 98% and 99% in 2015, respectively. However, the trend is much less pronounced in Scopus; there is a sharp decline in the proportion of English for the earlier years, followed by an increase in recent years. Although there are no comparable large-scale data for Google Scholar, preliminary evidence has shown that it has a strong English-language bias, which is due to its

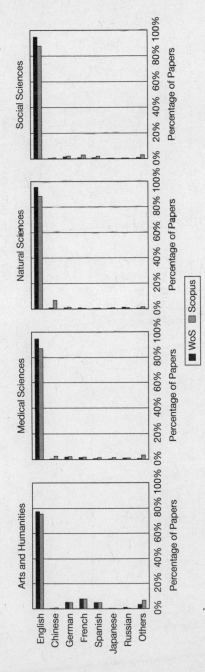

Figure 2.3 Percentage of Scopus (1996–2015) and WoS (1980–2015) papers, by language.

Source: Web of Science and Scopus, aggregated NSF disciplines.

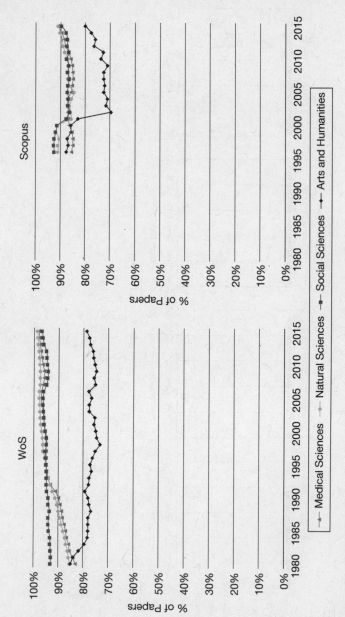

Figure 2.4 Percentage of English-language papers, WoS (1980–2015) and Scopus (1996–2015).

Source: Web of Science and Scopus, aggregated NSF disciplines.

exclusive use of online papers (and the dominance of English language on the Web). On the whole, these results demonstrate the dominance of English research in contemporary indices.

As with data on country of publication, comparisons among databases do not reflect the representation of language across the population of published literature. Using Ulrich's index of periodical titles for an estimation, it has been shown that Scopus and WoS overestimate English in all domains, and French and German in the natural sciences. In the medical sciences, there is a large overrepresentation in the WoS of Ukrainian research, with an underrepresentation of the same research in Scopus. Meanwhile, Scopus favors French in medical sciences, whereas this is underrepresented in the WoS. English is highly overrepresented in coverage in both the social sciences and humanities—to a greater extent than the overrepresentation in natural and medical sciences. These differences emphasize not only the disparities in language coverage, but also the need to interpret data appropriately, according to the database used.

It is often argued that, despite these disparities, the main bibliometric databases cover the most cited and, by extension, the most important works of scholarship. However, such claims overlook the importance of national journals, which often produce work that is of high local significance. For example, a large proportion of health sciences research in a country is conducted on topics of local relevance. This is a function of both the public service element of these domains, but also the availability of research subjects: A large amount of research requiring human subjects uses convenience samples, and there must be a sizeable population nearby with the condition of interest. This has led to an environment in which many health issues are published first in national journals. In addition, there are several other public service topics that have a uniquely local audience, given the variation among systems. For example, education, health, and public administration systems are often markedly different from one country to another, and are, therefore, of highest perceived value to others within that same system. Given this, many of the citations generated by these works are internal. Their international impact may be small, but their local impact is high. This speaks to the value of normalized indicators that take this into account as well as country-level resources that make visible this research. Along these lines, encouraging publication in international journals has the negative effect of reducing the dissemination of research on topics of local and national interest, mainly because international journals are much less likely to publish articles with local themes.

Several localized datasets have emerged in recent years, with the goal of making research from a particular country or given domain accessible. For example, SciELO in Brazil has made great strides in terms of local coverage, providing a far more comprehensive set of research journals for Brazil—as well as for Latin America and parts of Africa—than is available in the WoS. Unfortunately, citation indices work best at scale; that is, one needs not only a specific population of coverage, but all the documents that are cited. In the WoS, for example, 75% of the referenced items are also indexed in the database (i.e., source items). In contrast, local citation indices have a much lower coverage of source items given their size. These sets, therefore, are useful for measuring production within a local context, but are less appropriate for generating impact indicators. However, merging local sources with more global sets (e.g., the WoS) provides a good opportunity to contextualize local coverage in the broader impact space. Such integration into larger citation indices is currently underway for some of these datasets. For example, Clarivate partnered with SciELO to merge this source with the WoS. This is a symbiotic relationship, in that the WoS can market higher international coverage and SciELO can meet its mission of making Brazilian and Latin American science more visible.

How are disciplines defined?

Disciplines are key units of analysis in measuring research. There is a tremendous body of literature defining and debating what constitutes a discipline. In the broadest terms, disciplines are seen as a community of scholars, organized around a particular knowledge domain, with an infrastructure for researching and disseminating knowledge. Components of that infrastructure include educational curricula and programs as well as venues for communication, such as journals. For the purpose of evaluating research, subject classifications largely serve as proxies for disciplines. Disciplinary classifications need to represent meaningful units for a given set of researchers. Most classification systems present disciplinary units that are parallel to academic units or share nomenclature with large conferences or journals in the field. If the unit of analysis is too small, it is unrecognizable. Too large, and it is nonsensical for evaluation. This is the Goldilock's problem of measuring research: The unit of analysis needs to be just right. Interpretation and normalization depend on it.

Many different classification and categorization systems exist. For example, the WoS and Scopus both have their own categorization systems for journals, utilizing indexer- and publisher-supplied keywords and other material. The National Science Foundation provides a classification of disciplines for educational purposes. ProQuest provides a classification system for dissertations and theses. The Library of Congress and other library taxonomies provide classification systems for books. MeSH headings organize biomedical research through a keyword-based classification system. In research evaluation, the validity of these classification systems is imperative for field-normalization, for discipline-specific analyses, as well as for benchmarking and comparisons. Like all other indicators, the validity of the indicator is determined by the closeness to which it represents the concept it measures. In this case, the degree to which the disciplinary classification system represents the structure of knowledge and the accuracy with which units are placed into these disciplines determines validity.

The vast majority of disciplinary classifications in research measurement occurs at the journal level, and both the WoS and Scopus assign one or several disciplines to the journals they index. The WoS employs two different schemes: one by research area and the other by subject category. The first scheme divides the world of research into five broad categories and 151 disciplines; the second divides journals into 252 subject categories. Research areas are attributed to all resources in the WoS; subject categories—which are more precise—are limited to the information provided in the core collection of the WoS.

Scopus uses a similar classification scheme. It categorizes journals into four broad categories—labeled clusters—then into 27 major subject areas, which is further subdivided into more than 300 minor subject areas. For both Scopus and WoS classifications, journals may be categorized into more than one category. Although Google Scholar does not provide any discipline information in its search results—a feature it has lost over the years—it does contain a field classification of journals, which is used for the construction of journal citation indicators. No details, however, are presented on the method used for the categorization.

When comparing data or using multiple data sources in a single investigation, it is often necessary to merge or overlay classification systems. This interoperability is fairly easily achieved for journals due to standard journals names or direct identifiers associated with each journal (i.e., the ISSN), which serve as cross-walking mechanisms. This is one utility of a journal-based classification system. The other is the relative stasis of the classification system, which allows for historical and trend analysis.

However, there are several drawbacks to disciplinary classifications at the journal level. The most critical is that the journal is not always the best proxy for the content of the paper. For example, in the case of *Science* and *Nature*, these journals are attributed to all disciplines in Scopus and classified as multidisciplinary journals in the WoS. This tells us little about the actual papers and how they relate and contribute to other disciplines. Furthermore, the same situation can be seen *within* disciplines: the *Journal of the American Chemical Society*, for example, will publish in polymer chemistry, organic chemistry, geochemistry, agrochemicals, etc. Each of these subfields of chemistry has different citation practices and there are inequalities when these data are collapsed for the purpose of measuring research, given that some specialties are more productive or have higher average citation rates than others.

Normalization depends on homogeneity: Too much heterogeneity among the units leads to distortion and displacement of certain subfields. In turn, this leads to disparities in perceptions of performance and relative merit. Take, for example, the Research Excellence Framework in the United Kingdom. Imagine a group of scholars that has high production and citation impact and is classed in the mathematical sciences. This unit will appear to be the most productive and will receive a greater share of resources. However, one might subsequently decide that some of these units should actually be classed in computer science and informatics. In this case, with the same production and impact, the same scholars will be only moderately productive and cited relative to the new set of peer units and, thus, receive fewer resources. There are, therefore, direct implications for the classification of units and individuals into disciplines.

Disciplines also need to have some relative stability over time. This can be difficult, as some disciplines evolve at a much faster rate than others. Measurement depends on standard parameters for comparison. With too much dynamicity, it is difficult to assess trends or create comparative indicators. There is also variation in the level of aggregation provided by field, depending on both production and coverage. For example, in the WoS and Scopus field delineation, physics is broken down into several subfields whereas sociology is not—despite both disciplines being equivalent in most university structures (i.e., departments). Taken globally, field classifications within citation indices contain more granularity within the natural and medical sciences than the social sciences and humanities. This means that normalization for the latter is far less precise.

As noted earlier, each platform has its own way of classifying disciplines. This is largely because disciplinary schemas were created for retrieval purposes rather than for research evaluation. Therefore, it can be very difficult to measure research across multiple genres and evaluate the consistency and validity of these classification systems. However, appropriate research policy often depends on understanding not only the production of some units, but on the relationship among units (e.g., doctoral graduates in a field with research production in this field).

It might also be of interest for academic administrators to rank a given individual within a discipline. In these cases, it is typical to use the unit with which they associate or the journals in which they publish as proxies for the individual's disciplinary orientation. However, this can lead to serious distortions, particularly for individuals who are active in more than one discipline. Categorization schemes are often premised on the notion of exclusivity; that is, each unit is placed in a single discipline. This can be problematic for highly interdisciplinary areas of research and does not accurately represent contemporary science.

This tension between exclusivity and interdisciplinarity is often resolved by using document-level classifications. Document-level classification systems can be based on documents' referencing patterns or the content provided by abstracts, titles, or keywords. These data are mined to improve the classification of articles into specialties, to conduct scientific forecasting, and to explore interdisciplinarity from a new vantage point, among other things. Developments in topic analysis and clustering techniques have led to increased availability of document-level disciplinary classifications. These are not without limitations, however. The approaches require high computing power, access to good metadata, and, in many cases, access to the full-text of articles.

An inductive approach to disciplinary classification at the document level—which is constructed computationally and relationally and thus changes with each new year of data—is useful for identifying trends, but creates problems when one needs to measure research over time with stable categories. Furthermore, the results are often difficult to interpret: some analyses have produced more than 20,000 subfields—far too many for meaningful analytical distinctions. Also, given that the subfields are identified computationally based on similarities of documents, the labeling is provided post-hoc and manually. The number of subfields revealed makes labeling not only incredibly time consuming, but nearly impossible to construct, as it requires in-depth knowledge of all specialties of science. Furthermore, given that the distinctions emerge from the data, clusters will be differently structured for high citation density than lower citation density fields; for example, medical sciences will appear fragmented, while social sciences will appear as a large cluster. This does not reflect our knowledge of actual research or organizational structures for these fields and is difficult to translate to a broader community. In sum, mapping the literature using document-based approaches presents accurate state-of-the-art renderings, but is often structurally, epistemologically, or sociologically incoherent. Journal-level classifications provide more coherent classifications that model onto most scholars' understandings of the knowledge space.

3

THE INDICATORS

How is authorship defined and measured?

Authorship is at the heart of bibliometric indicators: It is authors, whose names and institutions appear on a document, who are measured. Historically, the term *author* was synonymous with writer. In contemporary parlance, however, authorship denotes myriad contributions to research, including writing, but also capturing those who contribute to design, analysis, experimentation, or provide resources to support the research. There may also be individuals who contribute, but are not acknowledged as an author on the final research project. Despite these complexities, authorship remains the marker—and thus the measurable attribute—of the concept of contribution to research.

Authorship attribution practices vary by discipline. The classical notion of authorship can be found in the arts, humanities, and most of the social sciences; that is, authorship is indistinguishable from the act of writing. In these disciplines, writing is the contribution that garners authorship, whereas technical and other types of work often go unrewarded through authorship. As a consequence of both the mode of inquiry and these authorship practices, author lists tend to be shorter in these disciplines. Differences in authorship attribution are seen not only at the discipline level, but also across specialties and continents. For example, if one compares sociologists in France and the United States, shorter author lists and more qualitative work can be found in France, whereas American sociologists are more likely to do quantitative work and, subsequently, have more authors on the byline.

High energy physics is at the most extreme end of the authorship spectrum. For example, there are standard author lists for research produced at CERN—the European Organization for Nuclear Research—which includes every senior researcher who devotes at least 50% of his time to research, as well as all doctoral and postdoctoral students who contribute 100% of their time. These authors remain on the standard author list for 1 year after they leave CERN. Although an author can withdraw his name from a given publication, they are included by default. It is important to note that, in these large-scale collaborations, authors' names are written in alphabetical order, which makes it impossible from the byline of articles to determine the relative contribution of individual authors. The peculiarity of this authorship attribution practice is due to the complex nature of the technical apparatus, which needs the contribution of hundreds, if not thousands, of individuals. This magnitude is best demonstrated by a publication in 2015, which listed more than 5,000 authors. Of the 33-page article, 24 pages are dedicated to listing the authors. Such expansive author lists demonstrate the complexity of the dual role played by authorship: both to provide credit for contribution, but also to assign responsibility for the research.

Laboratory-based disciplines are often collaborative as well, though not at the scale of high energy physics. In these disciplines, information about contribution is often implied in the ordering of authorship lists. For example, one would expect the first author listed to be the individual who performed most of the work (and is often a doctoral or postdoctoral student), whereas the last author is typically the head of the lab or another established researcher who contributed conceptual work but may not have been involved with the experimentation. Middle authors are largely lab technicians, students, or other collaborators who were associated with a single task—such as doing the experiment or contributing reagents. Thus, the status and contribution are implicitly embedded in the order.

Authorship order, however, has become an increasingly imprecise indicator of contribution as authorship lists increase. This has given rise to the concept and measurement of contributorship, in which the contribution to the article is made explicit—not unlike the credits appearing at the end of a movie. Many journals have established practices of recording these data in the acknowledgments or in another specially designated section of the article. However, contributorship data are often buried in .pdfs, making any large-scale systematic analysis—and, thereby, construction of indicators—largely impossible. There has been a shift in recent years, however, as journals have begun to collect and display this information alongside other metadata. In doing so, one can measure not only how many articles were authored by a given individual, but the exact nature of the contribution of an author to a body of work. The formation of the CRediT taxonomy and the adoption of this taxonomy for contributorship by PLOS journals should facilitate movement to collect and construct indicators on the basis of contributorship. However, given that contributorship is not indexed in large-scale databases (as is authorship), contributorship remains a concept lacking an indicator.

Despite standards in authorship—such as those of the International Committee of Medical Journal Editors—unethical authorship practices persist. The two most well-known abuses are ghost authorship and honorific authorship. Ghost authorship is when an author contributes to the scholarship, but is not listed on the byline of the article. In this situation, credit is not given where it is due. Honorific authorship represents the inverse, where someone is credited for authorship, but either did no work or insufficient work to warrant authorship. Identifying ghost and honorific authorship is complicated by the variation in disciplinary practices in authorship. For example, in history, an author may have received significant research support by a doctoral student who is credited in the acknowledgment section but not credited with authorship. A similar level of contribution on an article in sociology, for instance, might warrant authorship on the article. There are also inequalities in how authorship criteria are established and applied between individuals at various ranks in the scientific hierarchy. For example, a more substantial amount of work may be required for a doctoral student to warrant authorship, whereas a small investment from an established researcher will manifest itself in terms of authorship credit. This inequality plays into the Matthew and Matilda effects (see chapter 1) which leads to cumulative advantages for senior scholars and disparities for junior researchers and women, as well as those in temporary positions. Large-scale collection of contributorship data may lessen these unethical practices, as authors will be required to be more explicit about how labor is distributed for research production.

How is research production defined and measured?

Research production is defined as the amount of published output—such as journal articles, books, and conference papers—of various research units. In this conceptualization, the higher the output produced by an individual or research unit, the greater perceived level of research production in that unit. As an indicator, research production is precisely what it purports to be: a measurement of output, rather than quality. This becomes conflated when research production is valorized, absent other context. When research production indicators are used as the basis of awards or other recognition, production is incentivized. In many cases, this is a desired outcome. For example, an institution may be interested in identifying areas of high research activity within their organization or examining whether increased activity in a particular area was the result of targeted investment. For these purposes, research production indicators may be informative.

Researchers communicate their work in a variety of ways. Books, journal articles, and conference papers have long served as dominant forms of research dissemination. Letters to the editors and reviews provide documentation of interaction among scholars. Increasingly, scholars are making available data and other nontextual sources of scholarship, widening the body of available knowledge production. Measurement of research production, however, is typically limited to research articles and reviews—historically considered in the Web of Science (WoS) as *citable items*—as well as conference proceedings and books, in cases where these documents are indexed. This is a noted limitation of production indicators.

The simplest method for measuring research production is the full counting of scholarly publications, which attributes one "article unit" to each entity (author, institution, country, etc.) appearing on a scholarly article. This is equivalent to counting the number of publications in a CV: At the individual level, researchers are credited for each publication on which they are an author. The same applies to higher levels of aggregation, wherein each center, institution, or country receives one full count for each publication with which the unit is affiliated. However, full counting methods lead to an inflated perception of actual output: Due to collaboration, the sum of the full counts of articles of individual researchers (or any level of aggregation) will always exceed the actual number of distinct documents produced by the group of researchers (or any other higher level of aggregation). For instance, while there are slightly more than 2 million documents indexed in the WoS for 2015, they contain more than 5.2 million institutional addresses and more than 10 million authors, demonstrating the extent of the inflation associated with full counting of scholarly publications. This inflation creates a gap between the concept of research production and the indicator, as it overestimates the contribution of each entity to the unit of knowledge produced. This method may also contribute to unethical authorship practices (e.g., honorific authorship) as the placement of authors on the byline comes at no additional cost to co-authors. Despite these issues, the full counting method is the dominant method in bibliometric reports and systems, mainly because of its simplicity. Results of this indicator should be interpreted as the number of articles to which a given unit *contributed*.

Fractional counting, in which each author is attributed a fraction of the article corresponding to their share of all authorships, is an alternative to full counting. For example, on an article with three authors, each author would be credited with one third of an article; the same applies to institutions, countries, or any level of aggregation. The advantage of fractional counting is that the sum of articles of all units in the system is equal to the actual output in the system. The interpretation of the results obtained, however, can be more difficult. For instance, a score of 33 fractionalized articles might be the result of 33 sole-authored articles or of 330 articles on which, on average, there were 10 authors. Each scenario leads to markedly different interpretations of research production: Fractional counting provides an indication of proportional contribution, but does not provide an indication of how many articles were produced. Thus, triangulating both fractional and full counting allows for a better understanding of production and, to a certain extent, collaboration.

A limitation of both full and fractionalized counting is that they assume authors contribute equally to producing scholarship. Harmonic counting, on the other hand, assumes that author order is correlated with degree of contribution, with the first author being credited with the highest degree of contribution. Harmonic counting provides the first author with the largest fraction of productivity and gives to each subsequent author a fraction of the share of authorship received by the first; the third author with a fraction of that of the second, etc. While this begins to account for disproportionate contribution to work, it fails to take into account the dominant role played by the last author, who is often the principal investigator and corresponding author for the work.

Many bibliometric indicators acknowledge the dominance of first, last, and corresponding authors by only calculating production by these authors. Doing this, however, misses the contributions of many important participants in the research enterprise. Neither harmonic counting nor the use of dominant authors provides the total number of articles produced by a unit or their proportional contribution. Rather, dominant author counting is an indicator of leadership roles on articles and can only be applied for disciplines that use descending order of contribution for authorship and have dominant last authors.

All counting methods are highly correlated at the highest levels of aggregation, but variable at the micro—generally individual—level. There are also extreme differences across disciplines. Authors from high energy physics, for example, are disproportionately likely to contribute to more articles than authors from other disciplines, and to have more co-authors. Full counting measurements would be quite high for this community; whereas fractionalized counting would be quite low. Therefore, levels of production are highly tied to authorship attribution practices and must be taken into account in cross-disciplinary analyses. Given these disciplinary differences, one cannot compare production levels without normalizing by discipline.

As with any bibliometric indicator, research production indicators are dependent upon the data sources used to compile them. For example, using an analysis of the WoS, one might conclude that 27.7% of the world's scholarly documents are from the United States and 14.6% from China. There might be slight variation in Scopus (e.g., 22.5% US and 15.9% China). However, it is important to remember that counting these documents is the indicator of knowledge indexed, rather than the *actual* production of knowledge in China. For instance, there is a significant amount of research published in China that is not indexed by traditional citation indices. Therefore, these are indicators of production on the basis of indexed literature and should be interpreted as such. While an analysis of a CV might be able to demonstrate the difference between the actual and measured values, the scale at which analyses of research production are done requires the use of large-scale indices. However, research production indicators can also be calculated for a given unit using local databases that combine multiple sources to cover almost exhaustively the research production of scholars. Such databases have been developed and curated manually in countries whose research production is underestimated in the major bibliometric databases, such as Scandinavian countries.

Research production needs to be distinguished from research productivity, which typically takes into account the inputs in the system. For example, the research productivity of a university department could be measured by dividing the number of articles it published by the amount of external research funding it has obtained, or by the number of researchers in the unit. However, the use of these indicators must be carefully considered by administrators and policymakers, as it can lead to an inflation of productivity without a corresponding increase in quality. Therefore, productivity indicators are often used in concert with other indicators to provide a more comprehensive view of not only the amount of research produced, but also the quality of this research.

How is collaboration defined and measured?

Research is increasingly acknowledged as a collective endeavor. These collaborative interactions happen in many ways, both formal and informal. Informally, researchers participate in discussion at symposia and conferences and in the halls of academe. They exchange early drafts of work and consult with each other on problems in design and analysis, co-supervise graduate students, and exchange data and reagents. Formally, they may work together in a shared research facility or be funded on a joint research project. However, despite the various facets collaboration might have, measurable traces of these interactions are made visible when authors publish together. A document that has more than one author in its byline is considered to be the result of a collaboration; thus, co-authorship relations serve as a basis for the compilation of collaboration indicators. This means that other forms of collaboration that do not lead to co-authorship remain largely invisible from a measurement perspective.

Collaboration, as demonstrated through co-authorships, has increased across all fields, including the humanities (where sole authorship has been the normative mode). Several explanations have been given to explain this phenomenon: the increasing complexity and interdisciplinarity of research, the ease of collaboration made possible by increased mobility and a more robust technological infrastructure, cross-national funding programs that incentivize the sharing of personnel and resources across geographic boundaries, and the increasing expense of technologies in certain fields (e.g., high energy physics). However, it bears questioning whether the increase of authors on a byline is a reflection of an absolute increase in collaboration—that is, the number of people, institutions, and countries who contributed to scholarship. Rather, it may reflect a growing recognition—as well as accountability—of what Steven Shapin termed the "invisible technician" in science. For example, in biomedical research the number of authors has increased by a factor of six. This can be attributed in some part to the increasing complexity of the instrumentation and the need to collaborate with those who have expertise with these tools. Yet, it is also likely that there is a sociological shift in giving credit and responsibility to all those who labor in research. However, the assignation of credit varies according to the discipline, and this influences collaboration indicators and their interpretation. For instance, the counting of people named in the acknowledgments section of papers along with the list of named authors shows that social sciences' teams are as large as those of most natural sciences. Thus, the reduction of the concept of collaboration to co-authorship data alone may fail to acknowledge important contributions.

While collaboration indicators are anchored around individuals—that is, those who co-author a scholarly document—such indicators can be aggregated at several levels of analysis, based on metadata associated with the individual. For example, individuals are associated with particular departments, research groups, institutions, cities, institutional sectors, and countries. Individuals publish within specialties, journals, and disciplines. Any of these levels of analysis can be used for the construction of collaboration indicators.

A first group of collaboration indicators are based on the proportion of articles with more than one entity represented, for example, the proportion of articles with more than one author, with more than one institution, or with more than one country. Expected levels of collaboration vary significantly across time and by discipline. For example, the share of collaborative articles in the medical, natural, and social sciences has been increasing steadily since the 1980s and is approaching 100% in the natural and medical sciences (Figure 3.1; left panel). In the arts and humanities, a shift toward collaborative work becomes noticeable in the mid-2000s; however, collaboration remains the exception rather than the norm in these disciplines. Still, while proportion indicators demonstrate the presence of a given type of collaboration, they are not indicative of the size of teams.

A second class of collaboration indicators are mean-based indicators. These account for team size by compiling the mean (or median) number of units contributing to a piece of research. For instance, counting the average number of authors of a set of articles provides insights on the size of the team, while the average number of countries per article gives an indication of the international character of the team. As with any bibliometric indicator, more nuanced analyses can be done by incorporating additional layers of analysis. For example, a policy-relevant question might be not only how many

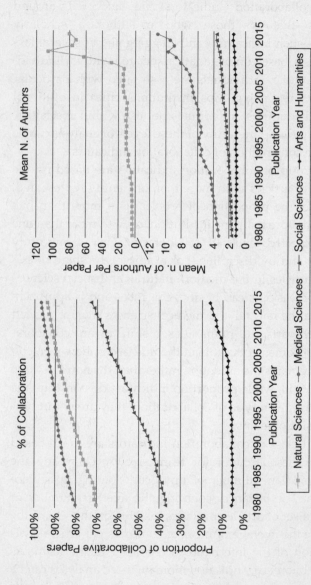

Figure 3.1 Percentage of collaboratively authored articles and reviews (*left panel*), mean number of authors (*right panel*) by domain, 1980–2015.

Source: Web of Science, aggregated NSF disciplines.

collaborative publications, but the proportion of collaborative articles that were the result of international or interdisciplinary collaborations. This requires high-quality data where authors can be matched to these variables (i.e., geographic location and discipline).

The mean number of authors is much less stable and prone to skewness from outliers. Certain disciplines and specialties drive the extremes; for example, in high energy physics—a subset of the natural sciences—the maximum number of authors in 1980 was fewer than one hundred. By 1989, the high was 500; it increased by a factor of five by 2006 and had doubled again—with a high of 5,000—in 2015; the effect of such outliers is clearly seen in the right panel of Figure 3.1. Therefore, caution should be taken to account for outliers and to be sensitive to disciplinary groupings when using mean number of authors as an indicator of collaboration.

One limitation of current collaboration indicators is that collaboration and co-affiliation—when a scholar has more than one affiliation—are generally not distinguished. Collaboration indicators assume that there is only one affiliation for each author on an article. However, there is a growing degree of co-affiliation, in which individual authors are associated with more than one institution (and therefore more than one geographic location). In this case, a single-authored article could be considered institutionally collaborative if the author is affiliated with two institutions on an article. However, more work needs to be done to understand and more adequately measure the distinction between these concepts.

Another limitation is the nonrelational nature of many of the indicators: They describe the degree to which an entity is collaborative, but fail to provide insight on the relative placement of this entity in the larger scholarly ecosystem. Advances in network analysis have expanded collaboration indicators to provide metrics of relationality—that is, the relations and positions of entities in the collaboration network. These methods are used to describe the centrality of collaborators in a network, at any level of aggregation. For network analysis, visualization techniques are central: Although centrality indicators (e.g., betweenness, closeness, eigenvector, etc.) provide meaningful information to the statistically informed, network visualizations have a potential to reach a broader audience and convey more meaningfully the relationships among several actors within the scientific system.

Collaboration and research production are intimately related; the authors with the most papers are generally quite collaborative. Collaboration spreads the workload, which leads to higher collective output, but the increase in output also has to be compared with increase in inputs. Using full counting (e.g., what you would see on a CV), the most productive scholars in the system are more productive than they used to be, as they manage to be authors on a larger number of documents, often as secondary authors or as head of research teams. However, when calculated in a fractionalized manner, researchers are less productive overall now than they used to be. This is a consequence of the differential growth of authors and articles: While the number of articles annually published has been steadily increasing, there was a steeper rise in the number of distinct authors, which has led to lower output per scholar in the system. This may also be a result of the increase in transitory authors on articles—that is, those contributing to a single or few documents in their career (e.g., such as students or research assistants) and who might have been omitted from authorship lists in previous eras. Therefore, what we see may not be a change in productivity, but rather a change in authorship practices.

How is interdisciplinarity defined and measured?

An increasing proportion of contemporary scholarship occurs at the intersection, interstices, and spaces outside traditional disciplinary boundaries. These activities are called interdisciplinary, multidisciplinary, or transdisciplinary. Although there is considerable discussion on the distinctions among these terms, they are often used interchangeably with interdisciplinary serving as the dominant term. Interdisciplinarity indicators are dependent upon disciplinary classifications. Disciplines are then overlayed on other traditional indicators to describe the level of interdisciplinarity in a given area, for a particular individual, or for a larger research unit. Common approaches are collaboration- and reference- or citation-based measurements.

In the collaboration-based approach, each author is assigned to a discipline, and the degree to which the output is authored by scholars from different disciplines is analyzed. This is complicated by the difficulties in assigning a discipline to a scholar, which can be done by departmental affiliation, though authors might change departments or have multiple affiliations simultaneously. From a bibliometric perspective, one can use the discipline assigned to the published works of the scholar or the journals in which they publish. However, many scholars publish across a wide spectrum of disciplinary areas. As a consequence, very few analyses have been performed on this level and most are typically of small scale with manually curated lists associating individuals with disciplines.

Reference- and citation-based analyses of interdisciplinarity, on the other hand, are fairly common, given the availability of disciplinary classifications of cited references. These approaches use documents, rather than individuals, as the units of analysis. Broadly defined, documents are considered more interdisciplinary when they make use of (or are cited by) disciplines other than the discipline of the journal in which they are published. Such comparison between the discipline of the citing document (or journal) and the cited document (or journal) make possible the analysis of several dimensions of interdisciplinarity. These indicators largely pivot around the notion of diversity, with the most common being (a) balance (citing different disciplines, but in equal parts), (b) variety (the sheer number of included disciplines), and (c) disparity or similarity (the degree of difference among included disciplines). All of these analyses, however, are limited to source items, as this is the subset of papers for which a discipline and specialty can be attributed. As a consequence, domains where a larger share of references are made to other source items—such as science and medicine—allow for the compilation of more precise indicators, while those where a smaller proportion of references are made to such items—such as social sciences and humanities—are much less representative of scholars' interdisciplinary knowledge combination. There is a growing interest in these indicators, but they remain within the purview of experts and, thus, are not provided in standard form in any of the current databases.

How is impact defined and measured?

Impact is a fundamental concept in measuring research and the Holy Grail for policymakers, university administrators, and funding agencies. However, impact is perhaps the most difficult concept to capture and operationalize. For the past few decades, scholarly impact has been defined as an effect upon the scientific community, as measured through citations. The simplistic rationale for this is that if one paper cites another, it demonstrates some form of interaction and engagement wherein the citing paper builds upon the cited paper. Of course, there is a sizeable literature on citation motivation, demonstrating a variety of reasons why people cite. For example, a citation may be used to provide background for a specific piece of research, frame an argument, justify the use of a method, or reinforce or refute a perspective. Due to these differences in function, some have argued that an individual citation is an indicator of *usage*, rather than impact.

At a small scale, there is wide variability and uncertainty in interpretation of citation metrics. However, at scale, valuable information can be derived. Simply put, if we believe in the cumulative nature of science—and least in periods of normal science—then the aggregate citation record is valuable in depicting the growth of knowledge. Each reference list is a statement on the landscape of knowledge used in a new piece of research, and those items that are continually cited are likely to have made an impression on the field. If a work is repeatedly invoked in subsequent scientific work, it can be considered to have an effect greater than work that is never or infrequently cited. In the aggregate, citations can demonstrate the cumulative impact of work on the scientific landscape. Furthermore, citations can reveal both strength of impact (by means of number of citations) as well as the nature of the impact (e.g., examining the disciplines or countries that cite the work). These arguments are more appropriate for cumulative than noncumulative sciences, which is why many caveats must be applied when applying citation analysis to the arts and humanities, as well as to some specialties of social sciences.

The measurement of the impact of science on the economy and society has been the focus of much contemporary debate and research by economists and sociologists, but has remained in the periphery in terms of standardized indicators. While some have argued that references made to scholarly articles in patents are indicative of the economic impact of basic research, this indicator remains technically difficult to compile, favors economic components of impact, and skews toward disciplines with strong technological dimensions. Proposed indicators for societal impact include citations of scholarly work in policy documents, newspapers, and textbooks. The growth of social media platforms—such as Twitter and Facebook—has led to the exploration of these platforms to provide an indication of the immediate societal impact of research. While social media metrics—often called altmetrics—are said to be indicators of the effect of research upon a wider body of stakeholders, their meaning is still being debated, mainly because of their volatile nature. It remains to be seen whether they are indicators of the impact of scholarly research on society—at least, in the sense traditionally employed by sociologists and policymakers. What is desired by science policymakers are metrics that can differentiate work that has high scientific value (e.g., major scientific breakthroughs) from those that have more immediate societal benefits (e.g., minor innovations that lower the cost of health care) and provide equal incentive for the latter. Initial research suggests that altmetric indicators provide more timely, but perhaps not radically different, results from citation indicators.

Many other concepts are often conflated with impact both in the construction and interpretation of indicators. For citations, impact is frequently mistaken as quality. For example, an article that has been cited more than 100 times may be assumed confidently to have had a greater *impact* upon the scientific community than an article that was never cited. However, we cannot say that an article cited 100 times is of higher *quality* than a paper that was never cited. A work may be highly cited for several reasons, including the contemporaneousness of the topic and utility for a broad audience. Ranking by means of impact indicators does not imply that an entity is of better quality than another, but rather that the work has received comparatively higher levels of attention and use—and therefore has had a greater impact upon science.

Similarly, in measuring societal impact, there is a high concern about equating attention with impact. For example, papers can become highly tweeted on account of humorous or popular content, but not necessarily have lasting societal or scientific impact. For example, the article with the highest Altmetric Attention Score for 2016 was a special communication in the *Journal of the American Medical Association*, tweeted primarily due to the high profile of its author: President of the United States, Barack Obama. It is clear that while there is relative consensus on the interpretation of impact measurements for science, systematic measures of societal impact remain elusive.

What is the difference between references and citations?

Citations and references are two sides of the same coin, produced by a single event: the act of citing. When an author provides a reference to another work, a citation is received by the referenced work; that is, references are made within documents, and citations are received by other documents. The distinction between the two is a conceptual one, but important for measuring research. First, while (almost) all research documents contain references, not all documents are cited. The second difference relates to time: References are always made to past literature and are static; that is, the reference list will never grow or change over time. Citations, on the other hand, come from documents written in the future. Therefore, citations are dynamic.

Despite being the result of the same act, references and citations are indicators of different concepts. While the use of citations for measuring the impact of scholarly research is highly utilized, the use of references is less common. However, references can yield many important insights. For instance, references indicate what type of research has been used to inform a particular body of work. This has many potential applications. For example, librarians might base their collection development on the work being cited by their faculty. The age of the work that is referenced is also important for describing structural aspects of science. For example, one could examine the bodies of literature that are relied upon, examining differences among populations, disciplines, institutions, or countries. There are some direct applications of this for measuring research. For example, the normalization of some indicators is reference based; that is, the denominator for field-normalization is the set of papers that cites a similar body of literature. However, for the most part, citations, rather than references, form the basic unit for compiling indicators.

Why is research cited?

The search for a theory of citations began in parallel with the development of large-scale citation indices. One of the goals was to develop typologies to describe the roles and functions of citations in scholarly documents. Several have been developed over the years, but the one with the most lasting use was proposed in the 1970s by Michael J. Moravcsik and Poovanalingam Murugesan, using articles from high energy physics. Their schema describes the function of citations using four nonexclusive dichotomies. The first delineates between conceptual and operational contributions, that is, whether the article is cited for theoretical or methodological contributions. The second delineation is organic versus perfunctory, which is used to describe the relevance to the citing article—whether the cited document is necessary for the citing document or merely an obligatory citation necessary to orient the reader. The last two categories are highly related: Evolutionary versus juxtapositional describes whether the citation builds upon the cited document or presents an alternative to it; similarly, the conformational versus negational axis describes whether the citing document confirms or negates the cited document.

The presence of negational citations was of particular concern in the early years of measuring research. Some scholars saw negative references as undermining the use of citations for measuring research impact. It was argued that authors should not gain citations—that is, academic capital—if their work was evoked only to refute or contradict it. It has been advocated that negative citations should be identified and removed from citation indicators. However, two arguments are usually used against this proposal. The first is the low rate of negative citations: Empirical studies have found, across various disciplines, that rates of negative citation range between 1% and 15% depending on the discipline and period studied. Furthermore, if the concept is impact, rather than quality, then the sentiment of the citation is fairly irrelevant. If something has been highly cited, even for negative reasons, one cannot ignore the impact that this work has had upon the field—propelling the field forward even if by refutation.

Taxonomies such as the one developed by Moravcsik and Murugesan, among others, were traditionally applied manually—that is, by a close examination of the text, inferring the function of the citation using various signals from within the text. One strong signal is placement within the text. For example, many articles in the natural and medical sciences are organized in the IMRaD format—that is, introduction, methods, results, and discussion. In this format, a conceptual or operational citation might be predicted from the placement of the citation: the former appearing in the introduction and the latter in the methods. Similarly, articles cited in the introduction are also more likely to be perfunctory in nature, whereas one would expect more organic references in the discussion. Placement alone, however, will not indicate whether an article is evolutionary versus juxtapositional, or conformational versus negational. For this, one must look directly at the text surrounding the citation. Several machine-learning approaches have been proposed to analyze citation context at scale, building upon the taxonomy of Moravcsik and Murugesan, but taking advantage of methods from computational linguistics and the growing availability of full-text data.

Citation indicators that take into account the context (and applied motivation) for citing can provide more nuanced interpretations of the impact of an article. However, indicator development in this area is still in nascent stages. More sophisticated studies of citation context are needed to begin to address these limitations of citation indicators and more fully understand the nature of the document from the way it is cited.

How do citation rates vary by time and discipline?

There are large variations in citation rates due to structural differences in science, including the discipline and speciality of the publication, time elapsed since publication, and the year in which a work was published. For instance, an article published in a discipline that publishes and cites large numbers of documents is more likely to be cited than an article in a discipline with lower publication and citation density.

More specifically, when there are more documents produced (either per person or in total) by members of a discipline, there are more opportunities to be cited. Documents published in niche specialties, with few scholars, or with slow publishing patterns have fewer citation opportunities. The cumulative nature of science also plays a large role in citedness. In areas that build directly upon previous work, citations will accrue more rapidly (and in greater number) than those fields typically considered noncumulative.

The extent of disciplinary differences in number of citations can be observed in Figure 3.2. For example, if we take all papers published in 1990 and indexed in the WoS, differences in citation rates can be observed as early as 2 years after publication and the gaps increase over time. For example, articles in the arts and humanities receive fewer than one and two citations per paper (respectively) across the entire period. Articles in biomedical research, on the other hand, average 7 citations within the first 2 years and 45 citations within 26 years.

Extraneous factors at the level of individual documents or journals can also affect citation rates. For example, language of publication will change who can read and, subsequently, cite a document. The visibility and prestige of the publication venue will influence citedness. Documents that are indexed in major scientific databases and published in open access formats generally have higher citation rates. The popularity of the topic, the novelty of the subject, and interdisciplinary appeal affect the degree to which a document is cited. A document that opens up a new field of inquiry is also likely to be cited more than one that solves a preexisting problem. Even the type of document (e.g., review article, methodological, theoretical) will change the potential citedness, with review articles being generally more cited than original research articles.

Citations take time to accumulate; therefore, time since publication must be carefully considered when calculating citation rates. On the day that they are published, most documents

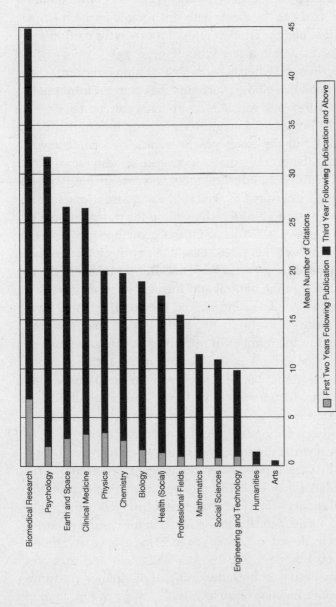

Figure 3.2 Mean number of citations received by papers published in 1990, for the first 2 years following publication and subsequent years, by discipline.

Source: Web of Science, NSF disciplines.

have no citations (although this is changing with the growing use of preprints). After the first year, rates of accumulation vary markedly by field, with documents in the medical sciences doubling the citation rates of those in the natural and social sciences within a few years (Figure 3.3). This is essential to keep in mind when constructing citation indicators: One should acknowledge how much time has elapsed from publication to analysis and consider disciplinary differences.

It is also important to consider not only how much time has elapsed, but the exact year in which a document was published. Citation rates have increased steadily across the twentieth century, mainly due to an increase in the number of documents published as well as the increase in the length of reference lists, both of which increase the potential pool of citations (Figure 3.4). Evidence for this growth is provided by tracing the indexed literature in the WoS, by discipline. Except for the decline during World War I and II, the number of documents indexed in the natural and medical sciences increased steadily across the last century, and the social sciences have increased since their introduction in the WoS. A steep shift can be observed in the number of references per document in all domains. Quite striking is the increase in the social sciences, where the mean number of references went from fewer than ten in the 1950s to more than 50 in 2015. These structural shifts contribute to expectations of citedness and must be considered when applying citation indicators over time.

These structural differences have led to an increase in citation rate, by year of publication (Figure 3.5). For example, for papers published in 1980 and indexed in the WoS, the mean number of citations received in the first 2 years following publication was 3.5 in medical sciences and 2 in the natural sciences; these rates increased to 6.6 and 5 over the next 34 years. Similar patterns are observed for the social sciences and arts and humanities, even if, in the latter group of disciplines, the number of citations remains fairly low (with a mean of 0.32 citation per paper for those published in 2013). The same trends are

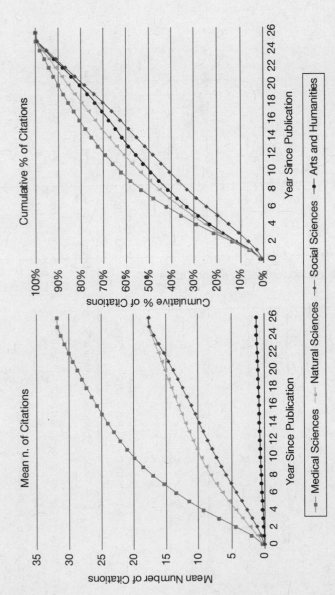

Figure 3.3 Mean number of citations received (*left panel*) and cumulative percentage of citations (*right panel*), by year following publication and domain, for articles, notes, and reviews published in 1990.

Source: Web of Science, aggregated NSF disciplines.

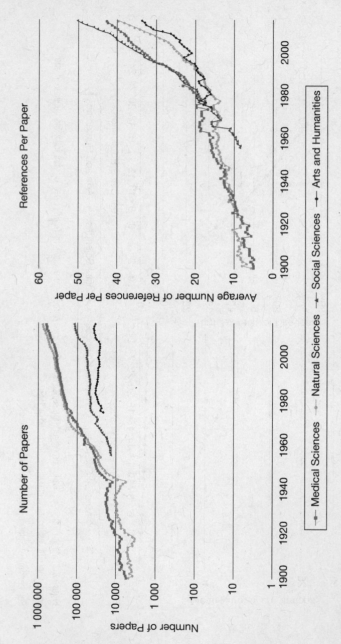

Figure 3.4 Number of papers (articles, notes, and reviews) published (*left panel*), and average number of references per paper (*right panel*), by domain, 1900–2015.

Source: Web of Science, aggregated NSF disciplines.

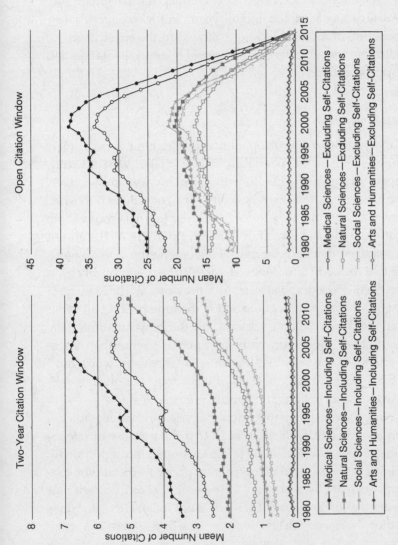

Figure 3.5 Mean number of citations received by articles (including and excluding self-citations), notes, and reviews 2 years following publication year (*left panel*) and until 2015 (*right panel*), 1980–2015.

Source: Web of Science, aggregated NSF disciplines.

observed with an open citation window—that is, considering all citations received—except that the gap between citations and self-citations decreases. This emphasizes the importance of self-citations in the initial years following publication. Therefore, caution should be exhibited in the construction of indicators that compare across years, taking self-citation and discipline into account.

What is not cited?

A 1990 article in *Science* opened with a damning lead: "New evidence raises the possibility that a majority of scientific papers make negligible contributions to new knowledge." The article reported that a majority (55%) of articles published between 1981 and 1985 in WoS-indexed journals received no citations within 5 years after they were published. The author emphasized that such journals were among the elite, suggesting that the body of unindexed knowledge was probably even less cited. He extrapolates from a previous study to suggest that 80% of the papers published in the time period had never been cited more than once and, on the basis of these data, asserts that "more than half—and perhaps more than three-quarters—of the scientific literature is essentially worthless." The many problematic aspects of this article demonstrate pervasive misconceptions surrounding uncitedness.

First, there is the assumption that scientific value and citation are inherently linked, that is, that the purpose of science is to get cited and that value is demonstrated through citation. This makes an uncited or lowly cited paper, as the author suggests, "essentially worthless." However, it should go without saying that the purpose of science is not to get cited, nor does citation exclusively determine the value of research. The scientific community should move from a pejorative to descriptive understanding of uncitedness.

Second, the article failed to take into account time in the analysis. Citedness is heavily dependent upon appropriate citation windows, which vary dramatically by field. To be cited, someone must have identified the article; incorporated it into their research; submitted the subsequent work to a journal; and have the work reviewed, revised, edited, and published. The review time in many journals is more than 6 months (or even a couple years) and publication backlogs can be much longer. Furthermore, the time that it takes to produce a piece of scholarship varies by discipline. One would not expect, for example, that a history paper would be highly cited within a year of publication.

The contemporary reality is that most papers in the medical, natural, and social sciences are cited within a few years of publication. Citations take longer to accumulate in the arts and humanities, but about a third of these documents have received citations within 25 years following publication (a conservative estimate, given the low coverage of source material in the arts and humanities). Self-citation has a strong effect in years immediately following publication, particularly for the natural sciences. Using papers published in 1990 as an example (Figure 3.6), we see that 55% of papers are cited at least once during the 2 years following publication when self-citations are included; this percentage drops to 41% when self-citations are excluded. These disciplinary patterns suggest that different citation windows have to be used in the various disciplines (shorter in medical sciences, longer in the social sciences), but also that citation analysis for arts and humanities—especially from a research evaluation purpose—remain largely problematic because of the low density of citations.

Uncitedness has decreased throughout most of the twentieth century. For instance, while more than 80% of medical science documents and 60% of natural science documents in the early 1900s remained uncited 10 years after publication, this percentage has decreased steadily and only a minority are now uncited. Documents are also cited at a faster rate, with a higher proportion of documents cited for the first time only a few years following publication. Uncitedness is

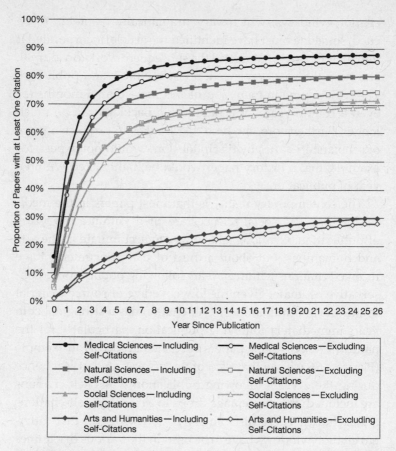

Figure 3.6 Proportion of cited papers (including and excluding self-citations), by year following publication and by domain, for articles and reviews published in 1990.

Source: Web of Science, aggregated NSF disciplines.

also dependent upon genre conventions in the discipline. For example, uncitedness rates are higher in engineering than in physics, a difference that is mainly due to the applied nature of engineering. Many applied disciplines publish their work in genres not indexed by the main sources (e.g., conference papers, trade journals, white papers, etc.). Therefore, coverage and citedness need to be carefully disentangled. Citedness rates are dependent upon the coverage of the citing items in the database used in the analysis. In the medical sciences, most of the references that are made by documents are to other documents that are indexed in the database. As a result, uncitedness rates are lower than in other disciplines. Uncitedness is higher in the arts and humanities due to the lower coverage of national journals, books, and other nonsource material. The invisibility of these items leads to conservative estimates of citedness. Therefore, not only are documents increasingly cited, but are likely even more cited than they appear given the nonexhaustive nature of citation indices.

How concentrated are citations?

Citation rates are highly skewed, with a few documents receiving the large majority of total citations. Figure 3.7 presents, for four broad domains, the percentage of documents that account for specific percentages of citations (Lorenz curves). It shows that, for each of the domains, a minority of documents are responsible for the majority of citations, but that the extent varies according to the domain. One popular rule of thumb for examining concentration is the colloquially titled 80-20 law, which, in the case of citations, would suggest that 80% of citations go to 20% of papers. This is actually quite close to what is observed, though it varies by discipline: 80% of citations in the arts and humanities are received by 12% of documents, in contrast to 16% of documents in the social sciences, 24% in the natural sciences, and 26% in the medical sciences. Part of these disciplinary differences is explained by uncited papers, which represent a sizeable proportion of papers in arts and humanities but a small proportion of papers in other domains.

The level at which citations are concentrated has varied tremendously over the last century, with an increased diversification in papers that are cited and, subsequently, lower concentration of citations within an elite minority. For example, in 1940, 20% of papers accounted for 80% of citations received; in 2005, this 80% was distributed across 40% of

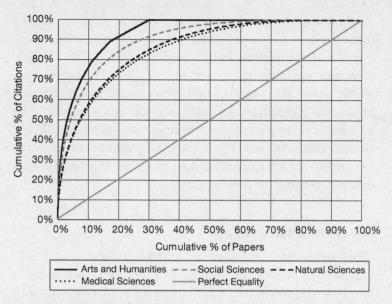

Figure 3.7 Pareto cumulative distributions (Lorenz curves) of papers and citations, by domain, for papers published in 1990. Diagonal denotes perfect equality.

Source: Web of Science, aggregated NSF disciplines.

papers. Deconcentration is also observed at the level of scholarly journals—the most highly cited research now appears in a greater number of journals than it did in the past. For example, while the *Proceedings of the National Academy of Sciences* published almost 9% of the world's top 1% most cited papers in 1986, its percentage of these top cited papers was down to less than 3% in 2010. Similar trends are observed for all elite journals (e.g., *Nature, Science, Cell*) and these trends are corroborated at the world level by a decline in the predictive power of the Journal Impact Factor. A decrease in the geographic concentration of citations received is also observed, which is mainly due to a diversification of the countries and institutions that are active in research and better coverage of the output of these countries and institutions. For instance, the share of all citations that are received by papers from the United States is decreasing, while that of papers from China, India, as well as other emerging countries is increasing. Concentration of citations, therefore, is diminishing.

How are citations counted?

Several approaches have been used to compile citation-based indicators, which span from the simple sum of citations received by documents to more advanced calculation methods. Before delving into the details of these various approaches, it should be noted that, at least in the primary bibliometric databases, citations are compiled in a binary manner: Irrespective of the number of times a cited document is referenced in a citing document, the cited document receives one citation. Although new tools—such as Semantic Scholar—are compiling indicators based on the number of times documents are cited in a specific document, the norm remains the binary approach (i.e., cited or not cited). While indicators of research production and collaboration typically rely on metadata—authors, institutions, journals, etc.—citation indicators require additional relational data; that is, references made by papers must be linked to corresponding articles and these data must be aggregated. MEDLINE—which does not index references made by papers and, thus, is not a citation index—for instance, can serve as a resource for the compilation of indicators on research production, but not citation.

The simplest citation indicator is the raw citation count, that is, the sum of the number of times a document is found in the reference lists of citing documents. Number of citations can be aggregated at any level, such as journal, institution, or country. The key question, however, is how to aggregate citation counts. While the skewed distribution of citations suggests that one should use the median (which is the value at the middle of the distribution)—rather than the mean (which sums citations obtained and divides this by the number of observations)— most citation-based research has used the latter rather than the former; as modal amounts are often one or zero and are fairly uninformative about the distribution. While this could be seen as a choice made by convenience—it is indeed easier to compile averages than medians—means have the advantage of taking into account all documents in the distributions, rather than only specific parts. Another issue with medians is that they tend to be very low, often close to zero citations. However, means are very sensitive to outliers: In such calculations, one document cited 1,000 times will weigh as much as 1,000 papers cited once.

One approach to addressing the skewness of citations has been to focus solely on one part of the citation distribution, and present data as a proportion of top-cited papers, such as the top 10%, 5%, or 1% most highly cited papers. The advantage of this approach is that it ignores the long tail. As a consequence, this method creates an incentive for scholars to focus on publishing a smaller number of articles with higher probability of citedness, rather than aiming for quantity. This calculation method has gained momentum and has been incorporated into leading indicators, such as the Leiden Ranking of Universities.

A similar approach is to transform the entire distribution into percentile ranks rather than using only specific parts of the distribution. However, given the difficulty of assigning a specific percentile rank (i.e., 1–100) to each paper based on its citation rate (particularly given the degrees of zeros for certain disciplines), these percentile ranks are typically compiled for groups of percentile ranks, such as the group of documents that are below the 50th percentile, followed by the 50th to 75th, 75th to 90th, 90th to 99th, and the top 1% most cited documents. Comparisons among individuals, institutions, and countries are measured by examining differences in the proportion in these categories. For example, an evaluator might examine what proportion of an individual's output falls within the top 10% of most cited documents. The same could be done at any level of aggregation. In this way, percentile categories combine article and citation data in a nuanced way, which allows for the examination of the performance level of articles, compared with success rates within a discipline, institution, or country.

Logs of citation rates are also used, which allow for the rescaling of citation counts. While this approach seems like a simple way to address the skewness of citation distributions, it leads to issues with uncited articles, whose citation value of zero cannot be log transformed. While some scholars have proposed solutions such as removing uncited articles from the analysis or adding a citation to each article, none of these have been widely adopted. Log transformations also have the consequence of reducing the importance of highly cited papers, which counterintuitively is the type of research one might want to emphasize and incentivize in a citation indicator.

At a high level of aggregation, these various counting methods are highly correlated. However, at lower levels of aggregation—such as individual researchers or small groups—the counting methods will produce different results. Such differences reinforce the importance of triangulating indicators—that is, using multiple indicators or high levels of aggregation—to strengthen the analysis.

As noted earlier, the discipline of the document and date of publication are two factors that contribute most substantially to differences in citation rates. Normalization techniques are utilized to address these differences. In the case of mean-based indicators, the typical normalization procedure involves dividing each document's citation rate by the average citation rate of all documents published in the same discipline/specialty during the same publication year, thus leading to citations scores that span between 0 and ∞, with an average of 1 at the level of the entire set of papers analyzed. Typically labeled as "relative indicators" or "field-normalized indicators," these citation scores make it possible to compare sets of documents published in different disciplines and at different points in time—such as the set of documents authored by universities or countries. Similar procedures are also applied to percentile-based citation indicators: Percentiles of citations are calculated based on distributions of citations within a discipline and a publication year, which makes it possible to compare percentiles obtained for groups of documents published at different time periods and in different disciplines.

Figure 3.8 shows that discipline and publication year-normalized citation rates are nonetheless correlated with raw citation rates—especially for documents with a high number of citations. However, the correlation is weaker for the subset of documents with a lower number of citations—at the discipline level, this variability can be a result of disciplines with low citation density; at the article level it could be an effect of recency. In such cases, the denominator (i.e., expected value) might be so low that receiving only one or a few citations leads to a very high normalized citation rate.

Citations can also be analyzed relationally, and this data can be used to construct networks of scientific entities. Co-citation and bibliographic coupling are the two most basic indicators of the relatedness between two documents. A set of documents are said to be co-cited if they appear together in the set of cited references of a given document. For example, article A cites articles B and C; thus papers B and C are co-cited. Bibliographic coupling, on the other hand, is based on the relatedness of citing documents: Documents are bibliographically coupled if they share a common reference. For example, documents A and B both make a reference to document C; hence, documents A and B are bibliographically coupled. These measures of relatedness can be compiled at several levels of aggregation. However, article, authors, and journals—as well as their associated disciplines—are generally the units for which meaningful indicators can be compiled. Such measures are used by retrieval systems to suggest relevant literature to users—in a manner similar to Amazon's recommendation feature—but also to measure and map the relationship between authors, institutions, and disciplines. From an indicator perspective, this can provide, for example, an indication of the centrality of a given author or institution

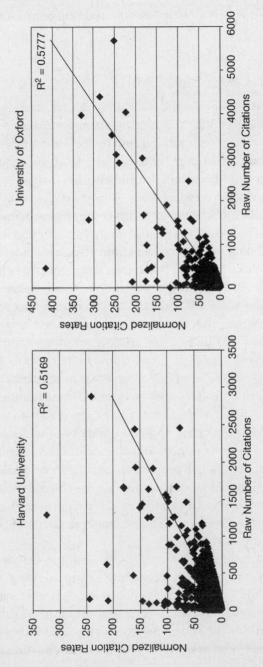

Figure 3.8 Relationship between field and publication year-normalized citations and absolute number of citations, for 2010–2015 documents from Harvard University and University of Oxford.

Source: Web of Science. Normalization performed based on NSF disciplines/specialties and publication year.

or the degree to which a discipline acts as a bridge to another discipline.

What are self-citations?

Self-citations and self-references occur when an entity (e.g., author, institution, country) receives a citation or makes a reference from or to another work written by the same entity. For example, imagine an author writes an article. In subsequent years, she writes additional articles and cites her own previous article. Her article also receives citations from articles authored by others. In total, 50% of the citations come from articles she has authored. These citations are considered self-citations. It is important to distinguish this concept (and associated measurements) from self-referencing. Self-referencing occurs when an author is in the act of making a self-citation; that is, when the author is writing an article and includes a reference to a work he previously wrote, this would be a self-reference. Imagine that ten of thirty references in an article are references to the author's own work. In this case, one-third of references for this article would be considered self-references. In mathematical terms, while both indicators are based on the same number in the numerator—which is the number of papers on which there is an overlap between citing and cited authors—the denominator varies between references and citations. Self-referencing rates are calculated as the proportion of references made to other articles authored by the authors of the citing article(s). The self-citation rate is calculated as the proportion of citations received by a given article that come from documents on which he or she was an author.

While the term "self-citations" is generally used as an umbrella term for both acts, conflating self-referencing and self-citation leads to inaccurate conclusions. Self-referencing describes how much an author (or group of authors) draws upon their own work to inform the present work. This requires having previous relevant work, which is dependent upon seniority, production, and a focused research agenda. Self-citations, on the other hand, demonstrate the impact of the work upon the scientific community. A high self-citation rate would suggest that the work primarily serves to inform the author's own subsequent work and did not have high impact upon the rest of the scientific community. These are two very different types of metrics and associated concepts.

There are several types of self-citations and self-references. For single-authored publications, self-citations are easy to define: They simply represent the citations where the name of the cited and citing author is the same. However, research is increasingly collaborative, and calculation of self-citations for collaboratively authored articles is more complicated. One can define a count of self-citation wherein there is overlap of a single author between the cited and citing author bylines on all articles. Other measurements consider an instance of self-citation when the first author of the citing and cited articles is the same. There can also be several other permutations (e.g., first author of the citing to any author of the cited, etc.) and multiple levels of aggregation (e.g., country, institution, or journal).

Volume is a factor at any level of aggregation, but functions in slightly different ways. At the individual level, a higher number of publications is typically associated with higher self-references. This is a result of having more potential sources on which to draw. However, the phenomenon works in the opposite direction when a discipline is used as the unit of analysis: The smaller the discipline, the higher proportion of self-citations and self-references that discipline may observe, due to the specialization of the field: The proportion of self-citations will be inflated in a field with a smaller number of within-field articles available for citing. The same applies to niche journals. From a purely probabilistic perspective, the more specialized the research area and the fewer individuals in it, the higher the proportion of self-citations and self-references one would expect to observe.

Both self-citation and self-referencing have increased over time largely as a function of the increase in number of authors per document. For documents across all domains published in 2000, they represent roughly 15% of references and 13% of citations (Figure 3.9), when one includes any overlap between citing and cited authors. Of course, this varies by discipline, with the social sciences and arts and humanities having a lower proportion of self-citation and self-references, and the natural and medical sciences having higher ones. These differences are mostly due to a higher number of authors per document in the latter group of disciplines.

Self-citations and references also vary by place of origin of authors and citers: As one might expect, at the world level, each country is more likely to cite other documents from the same country (Figure 3.9). For instance, while the United States accounts for 21.8% of all documents indexed in the 2010 to 2015 period, 58% of the references in US papers went to other US papers. Country self-citing is even more pronounced in smaller countries; for example, while Sweden accounts for 1% of documents (2010–2015), 20% of Swedish references go to documents authored by their countrymen. This can be partially explained by proximity—proximity increases awareness of work—but also from the perspective of national relevance. This is especially true in the social sciences and humanities, where research topics are often most relevant locally.

Self-citations are used as a critique of using citations to measure impact. Critics argue that self-citations unduly inflate citation counts and are fundamentally different from when citations are received from authors not affiliated with the cited document. It has been argued, therefore, that self-citations should be removed from citation indicators, especially when aiming at measuring scholarly impact. While there are indeed cases of querulous self-citers who disproportionately cite their own work, the act of self-citing should not be seen as inherently malicious. In fact, due to the cumulative nature of scientific work—as well as the trajectory of scientific careers—it

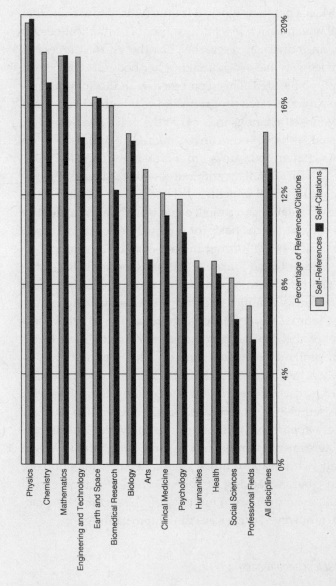

Figure 3.9 Percentage of self-citations and self-references of papers published in 2000, by discipline. Self-citations and self-references (as well as their corresponding denominators) are limited to source items.

Source: Web of Science, aggregated NSF disciplines.

should be expected that one would draw on one's own work. For example, if an author made a discovery or proposed a framework in a previous work, it is only natural to assume that this work would be referenced in subsequent publications. In addition, an individual researcher has the greatest access to and knowledge of her work, making her body of work much more likely to be cited. This, combined with the subject similarity of a single research program, makes it highly likely if not necessary for self-citations to occur at the individual level.

That said, self-citations can be gamed to inflate citation counts. As citation indicators are increasingly used to evaluate journals, some scholars and journal editors have been creative in finding ways to artificially boost their citation rates. Excessive self-citation is a practice that is fairly easy to identify and has been used as the basis for removal from citation-based indicators, such as the Journal Impact Factor. For example, in the 2016 edition of the Journal Citation Reports (JCR), statistics for 13 journals were suppressed due to anomalous citation patterns, such as citation stacking. Citation stacking occurs when one journal disproportionately references another journal. Some of this can happen legitimately, given high levels of topical similarity between journals. Malpractice, however, occurs when the citation stacking is done intentionally with the goal of increasing the citation rates of the journals. As with malicious self-citation, citation stacking between two journals is relatively apparent. More pernicious, however, are citation stacking agreements that extend beyond two journals. When more than two journal editors have agreed to intentionally engage in citation stacking, it is considered a citation cartel. Five Brazilian journals were found to be engaged in this practice in 2011; however, cartels are difficult to capture.

How is obsolescence measured?

The useful life of a scholarly document is not eternal. Obsolescence is the measurement of the decay and eventual cessation of citations to a document. Despite an increase in the number of references per document across the twentieth and twenty-first centuries—and the relative homogeneity of this value across science—documents in various disciplines are not cited at the same rate once they are published, nor do they continue to be cited for the same duration of time. In the year of publication, most articles are not cited, and it takes a few years for articles to reach their maximum number of citations. The time to peak is shorter in the natural and medical sciences than in the social sciences and humanities. Conversely, articles in the former group of disciplines become obsolete faster, while those in the latter group continue to be cited for a longer period of time.

Synchronous measurements of obsolescence measure the citations received following publication year. For example, one can take a given year and discipline and measure how long it took for articles published within that year to obtain half of the citations they received in their lifetime. Of course, because citations are cumulative, the citation window allowed for this is critical. For example, a 5-year citation window in the humanities would likely not begin to capture the full citation profile of that work; therefore, the median drawn from these data would be highly imprecise. Thus, to conduct meaningful synchronous analysis, an extremely long citation window is necessary for the humanities, which also means that aging properties of these documents can only be understood by looking at older documents.

Obsolescence can also be measured diachronically by compiling the median or mean age of cited *references* within a given year, referred to as the *citing half-life*. Using a 100-year citation window, the mean age of cited documents is around 5 to 6 years in the medical sciences, around 7 years in the natural sciences and engineering, and around 8 years in the social sciences. The mean age of cited literature in the arts and humanities is above 14, largely due to the use of primary archival sources, the non-cumulative nature of the disciplines, and lower reliance on data (which makes articles less prone to factual obsolescence).

There are several reasons why citation rates for a given paper decline. One explanation is the perceived or real utility of the knowledge produced: More precise measurements and descriptions of phenomena in a given discipline replace previous ones, scientific problems are solved and the research focus of a domain changes, or the truth value of a document is contested and found lacking. On the opposite side, it may be that the truth claims of a document are solidified and incorporated into the canon of knowledge within a given discipline. This phenomenon, called obliteration by incorporation, also leads to a decline in citations. For example, Einstein is rarely cited by contemporary physicists because it is taken for granted that readers are familiar with his work. In this case, not being cited is not a proxy for lack of utility, but rather *hyperutility*—the work has become foundational for the domain.

Contrary to widespread belief that knowledge is both rapidly accumulating and decaying—largely in response to the concurrent growth of the scientific workforce and rise of digital technologies—scholarly documents are cited for a longer time period than they used to be. In other words, the average age of cited documents in recent papers is older than the average of cited documents in older works. This trend has not been completely linear: the age of cited literature increased during WWII, decreased between 1945 and 1975, and increased again since then. The increase in the age of cited literature during WWII speaks to one of the mechanisms of obsolescence, that is, the availability and quantity of literature—less literature was published during WWII, and papers published during that period had fewer contemporary papers to cite. Conversely, post WWII exponential growth decreased the age of literature cited during this period. The fact that today's scholars are increasingly relying on older literature is due to a shift from exponential to linear growth, as well as retrospective digitizing, which allows more convenient access to older documents. The advent of online bibliographic databases—such as Google Scholar—which have performed retrospective indexing, are particularly important in this regard. This may also be one explanatory factor for "Sleeping Beauty" papers—that is, scientific papers that defy normal citation patterns, remaining uncited for long durations before being "discovered" by the scientific community.

Measurements of obsolescence reinforce the importance of meaningful citation windows for the compilation of citation-based indicators. While one can compile citation rates for recent documents in most disciplines—bearing in mind that these citation rates indicate the impact of documents at a specific point in time and that their relative growth or decay might be faster or slower than average—the citation rates are so low and the time to half-life is so long in the arts and humanities that the general consensus is that the use of citation analyses in these disciplines is limited.

What is the journal impact factor?

The Journal Impact Factor—also referred to as merely "the impact factor," JIF, or IF—is one of the most used, discussed, and derided scientometric indicators. It emerged in the 1960s with the first editions of the Science Citation Index and has, since that time, triggered enormous interest and scorn within the scientific community. More than seven thousand articles have been written on the topic in the last 50 years, with increasing intensity over time. The topic is not the enclave of scientometricians alone: The majority of papers on the topic are published in science and medical journals, highlighting the importance of this indicator for the entire research community.

The indicator is embedded in the WoS database—it was developed within this index and is dependent upon the data of the index. Hence, IFs are only available for those journals indexed within the Science Citation Index Expanded and in the Social Science Citation Index. Given the long half-life of citations (and references) in arts and humanities, journals indexed in the Arts and Humanities Citation Index are generally not provided with an IF.

The IF was originally developed to aid Garfield and colleagues at the Institute for Scientific Information to decide which journals to index in their bibliographic database, as well as to serve as a collection development tool for librarians. However, it has evolved over time from an indicator of journal value to researcher value; that is, the higher the IF of the journal in which a researcher publishes, the higher the academic capital of the researcher. The IF is widely used and has been shown to incentivize scientific behavior and lead to goal displacement, as researchers seek to place their work in journals of the highest IF. This has contributed to a growing sense of discontent with the indicator and proposals to eliminate or replace it.

At face value, the indicator is seemingly innocuous: Calculate the total number of citations received in a given year by papers published in a given journal during the 2 previous years and divide by the number of papers published over those 2 years. This should, hypothetically, provide one with an indication of the "average impact" of articles within that journal. Yet, there are several flaws to this calculation. The first is that journals publish many document types. Some of these are frequently cited (articles and reviews, labeled as *citable* items), whereas others (letters to the editor, editorials, news items, etc.) are considered by the WoS as *noncitable* items. There is, however, an asymmetry in how citable and noncitable items are included in the calculation: Citations for all document types are counted in the numerator, whereas only articles and reviews are counted in the denominator. This has the potential effect of artificially inflating a journal's IF when it publishes highly cited *non-citable* items, such as editorials and letters to the editor, which are, despite the label, actually quite highly cited. A good example can be seen in the case of *Science* and *Nature*, whose 2009 IF decreases from 34.480 to 22.770 and from 29.747 to 20.902, respectively, when non-citable items are excluded. This has led to gaming, wherein publishers have changed document types from citable to noncitable in order to increase their IF.

The calculation can also be manipulated by soft persuasions within the publishing community, for example, by journal editors and reviewers suggesting that authors include more references to the journal to which they are submitting or, in a more complex scenario, forming "citation cartels" and encouraging potential authors to cite other journals within the cartel. Journal editors themselves are also guilty of such manipulations: using references in editorial material within their journal to inflate the IF. The response from Clarivate Analytics has been to monitor and discipline flagrant abuses of self-citations. Despite these efforts, there remains skepticism within the scientific community on the integrity of the indicator.

Comparability of the indicator across disciplines is another severe limitation. Referencing practices—such as number of references per document and mean age of references—varies widely by discipline. The result is that IFs of journals in biomedical research, for example, will typically be higher than those in chemistry, physics, and most social sciences. One can even observe differences within a discipline, based on referencing and publishing patterns within different subfields. Hence, IFs cannot be directly compared across disciplines and specialties without accounting for these differences.

The relatively short length of the citation window in the indicator is also a cause for concern. Counting citations received over a 2-year period only captures a small proportion of all citations. The social sciences, where references tend to be older and citations take longer to accrue, fare much better when the citation window is extended. Even in biomedical research, where citations are obtained faster than in other disciplines, analysis of papers published in 1990 shows that citations received in 1991 to 1992 only account for about 16% of citations that will be received over the 20 years following publication. In order to take such differences into account, the JCR has provided, since 2007, a 5-year IF. However, the traditional 2-year IF remains the dominant metric and is often what is included in journal marketing materials.

Another important issue with the indicator is that it calculates a mean, which makes little sense in interpretation. A mean indicates that the citation rate is "typical" or "normal" for an article published within that journal. However, citation distributions are not normal: rather, they are highly skewed, with a minority of documents receiving a high number of citations and a majority of documents receiving the few remaining citations. In more scientific jargon, the distribution of citations is nonparametric, while the interpretation of central tendency depends on a parametric distribution. As a consequence, the IF cannot be considered to be an appropriate indicator of the typical scientific impact of papers published in the journal.

Several empirical analyses have sought to examine the predictive power of the indicator—that is, whether the IF of a journal is predictive of the success of an individual article—and have shown that, while the IF is associated with citation rates, this predictive power has weakened over the last 20 years. In sum, it is dangerous to extrapolate from an indicator of a journal to assume the value (or potential value) of an article or an individual. This indicator, therefore, should only be used as a journal-level indicator.

What is the Eigenfactor Score?

The Eigenfactor Score was developed by data scientist Jevin West and biologist Carl Bergstrom, both at the University of Washington. The Eigenfactor algorithm—which underlies both the Eigenfactor Score and related Article Influence Score (AIS)—leverages the power of the citation network, rather than relying solely on raw citations, to determine the importance of a journal in a given network. In contrast to other citation indicators, the Eigenfactor algorithm weighs a citation from a central source (in terms of network centrality) greater than a more peripheral source. The idea for this algorithm is derived from sociologist Phillip Bonacich who, in 1972, introduced eigenvector centrality to identify influential individuals in a communication network. His approach identified key individuals on the basis of their centrality in the network. The PageRank algorithm, the basis of the Google search engine, is another well-known application of eigenvector centrality.

In their introduction to the concept, West and Bergstrom ask the reader to imagine a scholar wandering endlessly through the stacks in the library, following one random reference in a journal article to another. The Eigenfactor Score is meant to represent the percentage of time a researcher would be redirected to a given journal. For example, an Eigenfactor Score of 3 would indicate that a researcher would spend 3% of her time with that journal, out of the entire network of journals: The higher the Eigenfactor Score, the greater the importance in the network. Given that the Eigenfactor Score is a percentage, if all journals are taken together, they add up to 100. In this way, the indicator is additive: to calculate for a set, the individual scores should be summed. It is not intuitive however, as scores obtained by most journals are below 0.01, and are difficult to interpret in the absolute. The Normalized Eigenfactor Score corrects for this by rescaling to attribute a score of 1 to the average journal. The Eigenfactor Score is calculated using a 5-year time window, in contrast to the 2-year citation window most commonly used with the JIF.

The AIS is more directly comparable to the IF, as it focuses on the strength of citations received per article. The AIS purports to have many advantages over the IF. In addition to the 5-year time window, which is more appropriate for many disciplines, the Eigenfactor algorithm reduces disciplinary distortions by relying on proportions rather than absolute citations. Furthermore, the Eigenfactor algorithm excludes self-citations—in the iterative approach, it does not allow for a journal to redirect back to itself.

Thomson Reuters added the Eigenfactor Score and AIS to the JCR in 2009. In 2013, the Eigenfactor Score was adapted to rank not only scholarly journals, but also the output of authors, departments, institutions, and countries (on the basis of author-level citation data). Six months after they are reported in the JCR, Eigenfactor scores of journals indexed in the WoS are available on the research project's website.

What is Source Normalized Impact per paper?

The Source Normalized Impact per Paper (SNIP) indicator was created by scientometrician Henk Moed, while he was at the Centre for Science and Technology Studies of Leiden University. SNIP is a journal citation indicator that claims to measure the contextual citation impact of a journal. The indicator pivots on the concept of "citation potential"; that is, SNIP operates from the citing, rather than cited, perspective by examining the average number of cited references per document within a subject field. Rather than using a predetermined list, the subject field is defined as the collection of documents citing a given journal. In this way, the subject field is constructed on the basis of an article, rather than journal, citation matrix. Furthermore, citation potential is refined by examining the context of the citation index—that is, taking into account not only the total number of cited references, but the number of cited references published in journals indexed in the database (which, in this case, is Scopus). Finally, the speed at which citations accrue within the field is also considered in the calculation of the indicator. As with the Eigenfactor Score and SJR, noncitable items are excluded. This reduces some bias, but fails to account for journals with a high percentage of review articles (these tend to have high SNIP scores). The advantages largely correct for issues in field classification, differences across and within fields in both coverage and citation practice, and the malpractice that can occur when noncitable items are included. Like SCImago Journal Rank, SNIP uses a 3-year citation window. Unlike the Eigenfactor Score, however, all journal self-citations are included, which can lead to distortion in extreme cases.

What is the SCImago journal rank?

The SCImago Journal Rank (SJR) was developed by Félix de Moya-Anegon of the Consejo Superior de Investigaciones Científicas and Vicente Guerrero-Bote of the University of Extremadura and continues to be updated and run by the SCImago research group at the University of Granada. As with the Eigenfactor Score, this journal ranking employs Bonacich's eigenvector centrality to calculate the prestige of a journal. However, in comparison with the Eigenfactor Score, SCImago weights links according to closeness of the journals, determined by co-citation relationships. The assumption is that two closely related journals—with greater transfer potential—are more likely to be topically related. Therefore, the SCImago algorithm increases the weight based on closeness and decreases the weight of citations coming from peripheral journals. The justification presented for this choice is that journals in the periphery are less able to speak with authority on the topic represented in the journal being cited (a contested assertion and potential limitation of the indicator). Journal self-citations are also removed, once they reach a threshold of one third of all citations received by the journal. SCImago allows users to examine the ranks of all Scopus journals using a publicly accessible web portal. In 2012, new enhancements were made to the original SJR. SJR2 uses a 3-year window, normalized prestige according to the proportion of citable documents, and sets a threshold on prestige transfer from one journal to another to minimize distortions caused by gaming and highly specialized journals containing few references.

What is CiteScore?

In late 2016, Elsevier's Scopus released a new journal impact indicator, named CiteScore. Based on the Scopus platform—which has broader coverage than the WoS—CiteScore covers more journals and takes into account, in a transparent manner, some of the criticism leveled against the IF over the last decades.

Contrary to many other indicators—such as Eigenfactor or SJR—CiteScore's calculation is simple, as it does not control for skewness of citation distributions or disciplinary differences in citation density. For example, the 2015 CiteScore of a journal is obtained by summing the total number of citations received in 2015 by all documents published in a journal in 2012–2014, and dividing them by the number of documents published in the journal in 2012–2014. It is thus based on a publication window that is 1 year longer than that of the IF (3, rather than 2 years). The simplicity of the indicator makes it easy to understand and interpret: A CiteScore of 4 means that articles published in a given journal over the 3 previous years have received four citations on average in the current year.

CiteScore tackles one of the most discussed issues with the IF, namely the asymmetry between the numerator and denominator. The CiteScore indicator does not discriminate by document type; rather, it includes citations received by any document type in the numerator and, symmetrically, sums all types of documents published in the denominator. Hence, while journals with a higher proportion of editorials, news items, letters to the editor, obituaries, etc.—such as *Science* and *Nature*—have "free" citations in the calculation of the IF (because only articles and reviews are counted in the denominator), these journals obtain a lower CiteScore, as such documents have lower levels of citations and are in the denominator of CiteScore. This creates an incentive for journals to publish little front matter. Critics have noted that this favors Elsevier's own journals, which tend to publish a lower proportion of front matter than other journals. This is particularly problematic given the conflict of interest: In the creation of CiteScore, Elsevier becomes a ranker as well as a publisher of journals.

What is the h-index?

The h-index was developed in 2005 by physicist Jorge Hirsch, whose goal was the construction of a composite indicator, at the level of the individual researcher, which would reflect both productivity and impact. The calculation of the h-index is fairly simple: A scholar has an index of h when he has published h papers, each of which has been cited at least h times. For example, an author would have an h-index of 10, if at least ten of his papers had received at least ten citations. Given the appeal of simplicity, the indicator was quickly adopted in many disciplines, particularly in the natural sciences and engineering, as an indicator by which the quality of an individual scientist could be assessed. This led to a so-called h-bubble, where several scholars in scientometrics and beyond rushed to describe the h-index for different populations and construct new variants. The h-index was also incorporated into bibliometric databases, thus codifying its use.

While the h-index aims at balancing publications and citations, in reality publication is the more dominant variable in the calculation, given that it represents the upper bound of the index; that is, one's h-index can never be higher than one's publication count. On the other hand, each additional citation—which makes a paper cited more than the number of publications of a scholar—is lost in the calculation. Consider, for example, the case of two scholars. One has ten papers each cited ten times. This scholar has an h-index of 10. Another scholar has authored five papers each of which was cited 100 times. This scholar has an h-index of 5—that is, half of the original scholar—although each publication is cited ten times more than her colleague's papers. As this example suggests, this indicator is also prone to scientific and sociological distortions given that it favors quantity in terms of publications (which is heavily affected by seniority, collaborative activity, and discipline).

Several dozen variants of the h-index have been proposed, many of which have tried to address the numerous weaknesses of the indicator. However, the more damning concern for this indicator is that it lacks an underlying concept; productivity and impact are two concepts that are integrated—and thus conflated—in the h-index. However, it is unclear what concept is represented by this composite indicator. Therefore, although many variants have been proposed, they all suffer from the same vice as the original—that is, the conflation of two concepts into one indicator.

What are altmetrics?

Citations have long been criticized for providing a limited picture of impact—that is, primarily demonstrating the impact of science on other scientific documents, almost exclusively through the lens of journal article interaction. In 2010, the quasi-monopoly that citations held over impact indicators was challenged by the introduction of *altmetrics*—a term connoting measurements of research that are "alternative" or supplemental to citations. The term was coined by Jason Priem, then a doctoral student at the University of North Carolina at Chapel Hill. Priem and other advocates called on the community to diversify ways of disseminating and measuring impact.

The most immediate source of data came from the social web, for example, tracing interactions with scientific documents on online social reference managers (e.g., Zotero, Mendeley, CiteULike), social media platforms (e.g., Twitter, Facebook), and other online repositories (e.g., Figshare, SlideShare, GitHub). Publishing platforms—such as the Public Library of Science (PLOS)—began to adopt and innovate in this area, collecting their own noncitation data to display at the article level (e.g., Article-Level-Metrics). Older metrics were also subsumed under this umbrella, such as journal download data (e.g., COUNTER statistics) and other noncitation data that were in the bibliometric toolbox before altmetrics was coined. However, despite the existence of noncitation metrics before 2010, the coining of the term in parallel with the rising use of social media for creating, disseminating, and discussing scholarship provided the fertile environment necessary to allow the concept to flourish. Within a few years after introduction, altmetrics broadly came to represent a heterogeneous set of indicators, whose common feature is that they do not utilize citation data.

Companies rapidly formed to take advantage of the growing interest in altmetrics. Three of the most established include Altmetric, Impactstory, and Plum Analytics. Altmetric was founded in 2011 by Euan Adie with seed funding from an Elsevier "Apps for Science" competition. It received continued investment in 2012 from Digital Science—operated by the Holtzbrinck Publishing Group (which owns Nature, Macmillan, Springer, and other publishing houses). The initial goal of Altmetric was to aggregate altmetric data for individual articles—that is, to trace the mentions of articles in a variety of sources, including policy documents, mainstream media, blogs, postpublication peer-review platforms, online reference managers, social media, and syllabi. Citation data from Scopus were later integrated into the product. The hallmark of Altmetric became the colloquially termed "donut": a circle of "flavors" that depicts, for an individual article, the sources that mention the article and contribute to the "Altmetric Attention Score"—a numerical indicator in the center of the donut.

Impactstory was founded by Heather Piwowar and Jason Priem. It began, under the name total-impact, as a hackathon project at the 2011 Beyond Impact workshop. It was seeded with funding from the Open Society Foundation and has received grants from the National Science Foundation and the Alfred P. Sloan Foundation. Impactstory draws upon Altmetric to supply all of the data on individual works of scholarship and supplements these data with data from Mendeley and Twitter. Impactstory is novel in that it presents the data not at the level of article or institution, but rather at the level of individual researchers. The assignment of publications to individuals occurs through ORCID, a researcher identity management service. This provides one limitation to the service, in that authors must both have an identifier within ORCID and curate their portfolios within the ORCID platform, in order to ensure accuracy of their profile on Impactstory. Crossref is used to provide additional metadata for the articles. Achievements— for example, scoring in the top 10% or 25% of researchers on certain elements—are provided by comparing users with a sample of more than thirty thousand researchers with ORCID profiles. However, profiles are not freely available, nor can one examine the profiles of others (as in Google Scholar). Rather, each individual can only access their own profile, upon logging in. Profiles are available for free (though this was not always the case), via a Twitter handle.

Plum Analytics was founded the year after Impactstory, in 2012, by Andrea Michalek, and aggregates data from more than 30 sources. As part of the EBSCO company (until February 2017), PlumX Analytics drew upon EBSCO library download and usage data, as well as holdings data from WorldCat. Data from Mendeley, GitHub, blogs, Goodreads (for books), Wikipedia articles, and Vimeo videos provide data on what the company called "captures" and "mentions." Social media platforms such as Reddit, Twitter, Facebook, and Figshare are all tracked. In addition to these altmetric sources, PlumX Analytics also draws upon citation data from Crossref, MEDLINE, and Scopus; clinical data from Dynamed Plus; and patent data from the United States Patent and Trade Office (USPTO). The company offers several products, geared primarily toward librarians and administrators. Sold to Elsevier in February 2017, Plum Analytics' altmetric scores are expected to be integrated into Elsevier's research analytics products, such as SciVal and Scopus.

Each of these companies provides slightly different indicators. For example, Altmetric includes references to scholarly papers in policy documents and Plum Analytics provides library holdings. They also vary in the level of analysis: Altmetric has historically focused on article-level indicators, Plum Analytics on institutional-level indicators, and Impactstory on indicators for individual researchers. The variation in data and categorization schemes leads to different ways of presenting the data; for example, Altmetric provides geospatial representations of the impact profile for each work, whereas Impactstory will inform a researcher how long their work has been trending on social media.

The sources also differ in data availability. Altmetric has made full data available to researchers; these data, therefore, are the foundation of most published empirical studies of altmetrics. Researchers can also download the Altmetric Bookmarklet to their web browser for free. This applet allows users to generate a profile for any document with a document object identifier (DOI). These profiles list the Altmetric Attention Score as well as a summary and details of all attention received by that work. In contrast, Impactstory only allows users to see their own profile upon logging into the system, and Plum Analytics only provides reports for subscribers. Plum Analytics and Impactstory have not released their data for large-scale external analysis.

One strong similarity among all the sources is their dependence upon unique object identifiers. Document object identifiers are prominent across the platforms, although several other identifiers are used (e.g., Altmetric uses ISBNs for books and follows platform-specific identifiers, such as those produced by MEDLINE, arXiv, ADS, and SSRN; Impactstory relies on ORCID for author disambiguation). This leads to neglect of many other document types and restricts measurements of impact to traces that incorporate these identifiers into the conversation. In particular, the reliance on unique identifiers obscures a large proportion of the conversation around research that occurs on social media without being tied to a DOI or other identifier, as well as the discussion of research in much of the popular press. Although altmetric companies are working to increase their coverage of these online activities, indicators to date remain heavily reliant on journal articles and their object identifiers. Therefore, altmetric indicators must be interpreted in light of this limitation.

A few indicators based on altmetrics have been proposed in the scientific literature. The most basic indicators represent counts and means of scores obtained by papers on these platforms: namely, coverage, density, and intensity. Coverage is the percentage of documents with at least one mention (or event) on a particular platform. Density is calculated as the mean number of events per document. Given the low coverage, density is often skewed by a large number of zero values. Therefore, intensity was introduced as the mean number of events of a set of documents, excluding those without mentions. Each of these indicators is calculated within a particular platform or genre (e.g., examining only Twitter mentions, readers on Mendeley, or instances of news coverage). There have been scattered attempts within the research community to create composite indicators, but these indicators have not found broad adoption.

One exception to this is the Altmetric Attention Score, developed by the firm Altmetric. The composite score is presented inside of the "donut"—a hollow circle of colors representing the nature of attention received by a particular work. Each color represents a source type collected by Altmetric (e.g., social media, blogs, policy documents, postpublication peer review, news, videos). The composite score is a weighted indicator of the attention received from these scores, amplified based on volume, the importance of the source, and characteristics of the source author. Volume represents the number of mentions from a unique individual and source—ignoring, for example, multiple mentions on Twitter to a single work from a single individual. Volume increases by each mention on most sources. The exception is Wikipedia, where the rating is binary: The score is the same whether the work is mentioned in one Wikipedia entry or one hundred. Not all sources are given equal weight—each source type has a specific numerical weighting assigned. For example, if work is mentioned on Twitter it receives one count; whereas it would receive five counts if it was mentioned on a blog and eight were it to receive attention from a new source. Some items are worth less than a point, for example, mentions on Facebook, YouTube, Reddit, or Pinterest. However, since the Altmetric Attention Score is represented as a whole number, the counts for each source are rounded up to the nearest whole. There are also weightings within sources, based on *reach*, *promiscuity*, and *bias*. Reach is calculated based on the real or imagined audience for a work. For example, on Twitter, the number of followers is explicit and the count is amplified as the number of followers increases. The size of the subscriber base of sources, like the *New York Times* is used as justification for amplification. Altmetric also examines the nature of past behavior of the author of the attention. For example, if a Twitter handle is constantly tweeting scientific articles, this will receive less value than a handle which does so less frequently (promiscuity). Bias is accounted for in the Altmetric Attention score by modification based on self-promotional activities, behavior associated with bots, and extreme outliers in the data. Despite this detailed weighting structure, Twitter tends to be highly determinant of the overall score, given the high coverage of documents on this source. Mendeley is also a source of high coverage, though Altmetric only collects Mendeley readership for documents for which a signal was obtained from at least one other source.

Altmetrics were initially proposed as "impact" indicators, in the same class as citations, and advocates and policymakers sought to examine the role of these metrics as indicators of the "broader impact" of scholarly research. However, early analyses suggest that the concept underlying these metrics might be more appropriately referred to as attention, rather than impact. There are traces of interaction, but traces that require far less investment and filtering than citations, for example. Those constructing indicators—especially the company Altmetric—have readily acknowledged the multiple concepts that are presented with their data, including attention, dissemination, and influence. Altmetric addressed the issue by going to the lowest common denominator: The Altmetric Attention Score added the word "attention" in 2016, in response to concerns that it was parading unjustifiably as an impact indicator. The current naming makes explicit that this is a measure of attention rather than impact. However, the composite nature of the indicator continues to be problematic: When the underlying sources of the indicator point to different concepts, the number itself becomes uninterpretable. There is, simply put, too much heterogeneity in the sources and concepts for altmetrics to be collapsed into composite indicators.

The use of altmetric indicators as measurements of social impact may also be problematic. Initial research has revealed that a large portion of those generating altmetrics (e.g., by tweeting an article or saving a document on Mendeley) are, in fact, other researchers. This is perhaps unsurprising given the reliance on DOIs: Researchers are more likely to be aware of DOIs and link to these in communications about science than the lay public. The public may be more likely to link to secondary sources (e.g., blog posts, news articles) or to evoke research results without a corresponding link. This is one critical limitation of interpreting altmetric indicators—as measured through DOIs—as forms of social impact.

Altmetrics are in a highly dynamic state: Existing tools change and die and new sources are constantly emerging, which leads to new indicators. Additionally, the same indicator can also be vastly different, based on the level of data access; for example, some companies will buy data directly from a platform, while others will make use of an API. What can be downloaded also changes rapidly, which makes replication of altmetric studies difficult. Citations, in a proper index, will only ever increase in number (only in Google Scholar might one see a sudden loss in citations). Altmetrics are much less stable. The Altmetric Attention Score, for example, can increase or decrease within a single day. The score might drop for various reasons: An author deletes a mention, posts are flagged as spam, the algorithm is reweighted, or data that were previously publicly accessible become private—such as Facebook profiles. A sudden increase in a score can be seen as new sources are added. The instability of this score calls into question the use of these scores in large-scale assessment exercises and impedes longitudinal analyses.

There are, however, benefits to altmetrics. Altmetrics add another lens through which the measurement of impact can be performed, going beyond journal articles as the sole source of impact. It demonstrates both broader elements of the production and use of science, that is, diversity in production and receipt. There is also the benefit of time, as altmetric data begin to accrue immediately upon publication and can be updated daily, or even more rapidly. There are great opportunities in this. Research can be tracked in unprecedented ways, and the traces of interaction that were previously invisible have been made visible. However, not everything that can be counted should be counted. In creating metrics around these online activities (e.g,. tweeting, blogging, and posting on Facebook), the behavior becomes incentivized and the data on these interactions potentially monetized by the platforms that collect them. For example, when policymakers incorporate altmetric data into evaluations they implicitly favor research of a particular type. This may lead scholars to seek topics that are highly "tweetable" and also to dedicate time to curating online profiles, rather than conducting their research. Altmetrics may contribute to an environment where scholars prioritize a taste for attention over a taste for science.

The expansion is, therefore, not just in data sources and new indicators, but the corresponding concepts that they measure (i.e., not just quality or utility, but also popularity or public appeal). Those measuring science should remain vigilant to ensure that each indicator is matched—and interpreted according—to a precise concept. The legitimization of these indicators is dependent upon their reception in the academic marketplace. At present, altmetrics have fringe status—acknowledged by some scholars, but not explicitly incorporated into guidelines for promotion and tenure and other policymaking initiatives. However, as funding agencies and institutions seek to find ways to hold scholars accountable for the "broader impact" of their work, altmetrics may become more fully integrated into the enterprise of measuring research.

How is research funding measured?

Funding indicators are available at two extremes—project and country level—with very few indicators available for meso levels of aggregation. At the micro level, most countries collect and make publicly accessible databases on the research projects they fund through their research councils. However, these data are scattered across agencies, and very few sources exist that integrate sources within a country or across countries and regions of the world. For example, in the United States, one can download raw data from each of the major funding agencies (e.g., National Science Foundation, National Institutes of Health). These data have been aggregated into a source called Federal RePORTER, a product of the STARMETRICS project, with linkages across many federal agencies and sources (e.g., MEDLINE and PubMed Central). However, the quality and comprehensiveness of the data provided vary widely by data source. Furthermore, these data only provide federal-level funding for a single country, omitting institutional or other internal funding as well as funding from large private entities (e.g., the Sloan or Mellon foundations).

Some corporations have begun to aggregate across countries and type of funding, and provide information on amounts received as well as number of projects funded. For example, Digital Science has created a tool called Dimensions for Funders, which provides funding agencies with comparative analyses of their research portfolios. Academic Analytics is another tool, which draws upon the various available datasets to create funding records for faculty members at higher education institutions in the United States. Despite these initiatives (all of which require subscriptions), measurement of funding is still highly localized at present. Creating a globally comparable dataset remains plagued by the isolated nature of these data, the lack of standardization in reporting, and the difficulty in merging currencies.

Funding is plagued with the same types of structural biases as other research indicators: It is highly field-dependent and skewed, with large amounts of resources concentrated on a few elite scholars. Funding data also suffer from precise allocation of credit, not unlike productivity metrics. For example, for some agencies, a single lead investigator is recorded, despite several co-principal investigators. When collaborators span international boundaries, it can become particularly difficult to understand (from the metadata alone) who is ultimately responsible for the work of the grant and who should be credited for the receipt of funding. In other words, funding typically attributes resources (or credit for funding) to principal investigators, and obliterates the increasingly collaborative nature of funded research.

Using funding data to measure research also faces several other challenges. One is the wide variability in the degree of competition for different funds. Although the acceptance rates vary dramatically—and have declined sharply in most countries over the last decades—funding is typically reported as a single monetary indicator, often with no distinction by source. There are also strong differences in a country's ability to invest in science and the number of candidates who are qualified to receive funding in a given country. Coupled with disciplinary differences in the need for and availability of funding, there remains high uncertainty and heterogeneity in funding, which threatens the use of this indicator as a measurement of excellence of research and researchers.

The Organisation for Economic Co-operation and Development has traditionally considered funding as an indicator of research activity, at the macro level of countries; that is, funding is not an indicator of output, but rather a type of input indicator, providing information on the amount of resources that are devoted to research. Of course, one would expect a relationship between funding and other output indicators, such as production and impact. However, this metric has evolved in recent years to be an indicator, at the individual level, of research quality; that is, the attraction of funding itself is interpreted as an output measure signaling the quality of the individual or lab that received the funding. While the amount of funding for a lab has long served this function in the sciences, it is becoming more prevalent in the social sciences and humanities where scholars are increasingly asked to demonstrate ability to attract funding as a requirement for tenure and promotion and for other evaluations.

The reversal of input and output variables can also be seen from the other angle, in that bibliometrics are increasingly being used as an input variable for the process of evaluating proposals for funding. Simply put, someone who is highly cited is more likely to receive funding than someone who does not have a high number of citations. Citations, therefore, are used to demonstrate credibility and to lessen the risk of providing funding to that individual. This is an inversion from using funding as an input indicator and calculating the effects of that input—or return on investment—by the subsequent receipt of citations. The creation of funding as an indicator of quality, rather than an indication of input, leads to many adverse effects, in which scholars who have no need for funding are competing for it as a signaling device.

What are indicators for applied research?

While basic research typically leads to peer-reviewed publications as outputs, applied research and technological development are often associated with patents. Like a scholarly publication, a patent is a written document that contains the description of a new invention, and it provides to the individual, or organization who owns its intellectual property, the monopoly over its commercialization in a given country. In other words, an inventor makes the recipe for an invention freely available, but has the monopoly on its commercialization.

Patents are granted nationally and evaluated by patent examiners who, contrary to those found in the peer-review system of other spheres of research—such as journals and funding agencies—are employees of patent agencies. Eligibility criteria vary from one country to another, but tend to focus on: (a) novelty (the artifact should not exist or have been previously described), (b) nonobviousness (US) or inventiveness (Europe), and (c) usefulness (US) or industrial application (Europe). Monopoly (or patent protection) generally lasts for a maximum of 20 years and annual maintenance fees range from a few hundred to a few thousand dollars to keep a patent protected.

The World Intellectual Property Organization maintains a list of all patent offices in the world, numbering more than 200 in 2016. However, there are three primary databases that are used to register patents globally: the USPTO, the European Patent Office (EPO), and the Japanese Patent Office (JPO). These three offices cooperate—as the Trilateral Patent Offices— in order to promote standards and share infrastructure. There is a hierarchy in patent offices, as assignees wish to maximize the extent of their protection and, thus, of their commercial potential. For example, Canadian inventors patent twice as much in the United States than in their own country. Hence, patents that have been registered with all three main agencies (USPTO, EPO, JPO) are labeled "triadic patents" and are generally considered to contain inventions of greater commercial potential. The importance of a patent can also be assessed with the number (and length) of the claims it makes, which gives an indication of the breadth of the domain covered by the patent.

Databases for each of these patent offices are freely available on the Web, to facilitate the patenting process; potential inventors and lawyers can and must search the registry to demonstrate novelty. Public registration of the invention is a critical step in the process, but also it provides an opportunity for those studying innovation to access data as the data from the USPTO can be easily downloaded. It is important to remember that patents in these databases are at differing stages of development; for example, the data provided by the EPO and JPO provide patent *applications*—this means that the data include patents that have not been granted (and might never be). The USPTO provides both applications and granted patents. This must be taken into consideration when analyzing patents, particularly when doing comparative analyses. Some databases provide aggregate patent data, such as PATSTAT, a product line produced by the EPO focused on search, analysis, and visualization of patent data. It boasts coverage of more than 100 million patents as well as 200 million status records from the mid-nineteenth century to the present. It aggregates data from 45 European patenting authorities and is updated twice yearly. The raw data it contains can be bought for a relatively small amount—a few thousand Euros—which is a fraction of the amount needed for the purchase of bibliometric databases such as the WoS and Scopus.

Metadata contained in patents are very similar to those of scholarly documents. However, notions of "authorship"—or inventorship—are slightly more complicated. In addition to inventors, who are the individuals behind the conception of the invention, patents also contain assignees, which consist of the individuals or organization who own the intellectual property of a patent. These distinct sets of names and organizations—as well as their corresponding cities, provinces, countries, etc.—relate to two distinct concepts: that of inventive activity (inventors) and that of ownership of intellectual property (assignees). Of course, while both are correlated—most patents are owned by entities that are of the same province or country as that of the inventors—this conceptual difference is important when constructing indicators. For instance, the applied research activity of a province will be measured using inventors, while the ownership of intellectual property or patent portfolios should be assessed using variables associated with assignees. It is also worth mentioning that, while variables associated with inventors remain stable after a patent is granted (inventors do not change), the property of patents might change as they (or their assignees) are sold.

Patents contain references, which means that patent citations can be compiled. Studies have shown a relationship between high citations and high economic value. However, the process of citing documents in patents differs from that in scholarly documents. One key difference is the involvement of patent attorneys and examiners in the process, who are seeking to demonstrate the novelty claims of the patent and, thus, might add references. Patents also cite very heterogeneous sources, which include other patents, scholarly documents, technical reports, catalogs, and websites.

Patent data can be used to construct indicators that are analogous to those created with scholarly documents. For example, one can count number of patents using full or fractionalized counting, compile indicators of collaboration among inventors or co-property, as well as measure indicators of patent impact, all of which can be broken down by technological classification or year. These can be grouped by levels of aggregation that are similar to those of scholarly publications, such as individuals (generally inventors, although they can also be assignees), cities, states/provinces, countries, and domains. Such indicators are typically based on utility patents and thus exclude design patents or patents for plants.

Patent indicators, however, have some limitations in their capacity to measure applied research and technological development. Some innovations are just not patentable. For example, software is not considered eligible for patenting in Europe and is not straightforward to patent in the United States. Other innovations are patentable, but inventors and assignees might prefer not to disclose the patent. Whereas the dissemination of scholarship is essential to generating academic capital, this is not always the case for patenting, as it is driven by another type of capital. Many firms might prefer to keep their invention or industrial process secret, as it might lead to more economic capital than disclosing them. This is the tradeoff for firms between patenting and disclosure: While a patent will provide a monopoly for at least 20 years—but increased competition afterwards—secrecy has the potential to last for longer periods. Patenting is also not always an indicator of commercialization. For example, some patents are owned by organizations not because they want to commercialize them, but because they want to prevent their competition from doing so. In these instances, patenting suppresses rather than propels innovation. Finally, one must keep in mind that patents have a relatively narrow disciplinary focus; while the measurement of research using scholarly documents can be applied to all fields—with the usual limitations of the coverage of data sources—patents only apply to a small fraction of disciplines, with the large majority of patents falling into two broad domains: electronics/computing and biotechnology.

What is the relationship between science indicators and peer review?

Peer review is at the heart of the research evaluation system. It can be broadly defined as the process by which scholars submit their research, proposed research, or body of work to be evaluated by experts within their research area. It is applied across several dimensions of the research system: It is used to evaluate scholarship for publication, proposals for the receipt of funding or fellowships, and at the individual level for appointments and promotions. Peer review has been the main method through which research and researchers were assessed, since the second half of the twentieth century. It is perhaps not surprising, then, that early bibliometricians used peer review as a gold standard with which to compare results.

Studies across time and discipline have consistently shown that number of citations and documents are largely correlated with other measures of peer esteem (with the former higher than the latter), although the correlation varies according to discipline, with higher correlations in medical and natural sciences than social sciences, and much lower correlations in the arts and humanities. This discrepancy suggests that these two approaches evaluate different dimensions of scholarship, particularly for some disciplines.

Despite these variations, peer review has begun to be supplemented and, in some cases, supplanted by bibliometric indicators. One rationale for the replacement of peer review with indicators is cost. For example, the cost of peer review for UK research councils in 2005–2006 was estimated at €196M, which represented 6% of the funds distributed that year. Furthermore, there are scientific costs associated with the release of several scholars from their research and teaching duties to engage in peer-review activities.

There is also considerable debate over the neutrality of peer review, with research providing evidence of both subjectivity and bias in peer review. While Mertonian ideals suggest that peer review should be strictly based on the quality of the research or researcher, there are many ways in which both explicit and implicit bias enter into evaluation. In contrast, it is argued that, despite noted limitations, production of peer-reviewed works demonstrate the capacity to successfully navigate peer review and citations provide "intersubjective" judgments of subsequent impact. While the relative merits of each approach can be, and have been, endlessly debated, it is clear that both approaches have their limitations at particular levels of analysis. For example, peer review remains the strongest indicator for evaluating individual researchers and smaller research units, where the domains are fairly homogeneous. However, science indicators become more useful at scale, when evaluating large numbers and highly heterogeneous groups of researchers.

It should be noted that there has never been complete independence between science indicators and peer review. Referees are not immune to indicators and, even when asked to evaluate solely on "quality," will often skim a curricula vita or Google Scholar profile to assess production, IF of the journals in which a scholar publishes, and levels of citedness. Even when these elements are not formally considered, they often find their way implicitly into assessments. This leads to inevitable correlations between peer review and science indicators. However, there remain strengths and weaknesses to both approaches, which suggests that these methods are best used in combination (an approach referred to as *informed peer review*).

4

THE BIG PICTURE

Who controls research measurement?

Scholarship is often lauded as a public good—that is, a product that is expensive to hold exclusively and whose value does not lessen with sharing. This notion, however, is challenged by the nearly exclusive hold of scholarship by for-profit publishers. The perversion of the system, in which researchers and their affiliated institutions must pay for access to their own research (often multiple times through overlapping journal subscription packages), which they have provided freely, extends to research measurement as well. The scientific community produces, but does not control, the data that govern it, and decisions about these data are often driven by corporate, rather than scientific, concerns.

Science indicators are strongest at scale. Two types of organizations are particularly well equipped to handle this scale: governments and corporations. Governments have largely focused on data about researchers and resources: surveys on education, the scientific workforce, and investment in R&D. With a few notable exceptions (e.g., the SciELO publishing platform in Brazil), governments have not directly collected publication and citation data for their scholars. The Web of Science (WoS) and, subsequently, Scopus emerged to fill this gap. The corporate monopoly over data on research production and impact has significant consequences for research measurement. Each of these companies has particular strategies and priorities that affect the coverage and availability of the data and functionality of the platform. Revenue is dependent upon library subscribers who primarily buy the tools for information retrieval, rather than research evaluation. The dominance of these tools as search engines, however, has been challenged with the rise of Google Scholar and other freely available sources on the web. The uncertainty of a continued user base may explain the sale of Thomson Reuters' Intellectual Property & Science Business—which included the WoS—to Onex Corporation (Canada) and Baring Private Equity Asia (China) for $3.55 billion USD in 2016. Elsevier, on the other hand, has responded to the competitive environment by acquiring platforms—such as Mendeley and Plum Analytics—and integrating the associated functionalities and indicators into their analytical tools, thus diversifying their portfolio and covering a broader spectrum of research indicators.

Market considerations shape the variables that are indexed and the indicators that are constructed by companies. In turn, these decisions set the standards for the research evaluation community. This is counter to what might be expected from a professional body: The experts conform to the tools, rather than the other way around. Take, for example, the compilation and promotion of the Journal Impact Factor (JIF): Consensus in the research community on the flaws of the indicator has led to relatively few modifications. Particular stakeholder groups also weigh heavily in decision making: The h-index—although derided by the bibliometric community—was included in all major platforms because of the coverage it received within the research community and the subsequent demand by researchers and administrators who, in many cases, are unaware of the weaknesses of the indicator. In other cases, providers can become producers of indicators, leading to obvious conflict of interests. For example, Elsevier's release of CiteScore—a journal indicator to compete with the JIF—was shown to favor

Elsevier's journals over those of competitor Springer-Nature. Along these lines, the recent indexing of acknowledgments by the WoS is restricted to those papers where funding is disclosed—rather than to all papers that contain acknowledgments—as such information, which could be monetized, is considered to be valuable information for funders.

Although there is corporate control over the raw data and infrastructure, there are a number of third-party research centers that have bought the data to perform advanced bibliometric analyses. Both basic and applied research are done in these units. Although they often sustain their research activities through contract work for governments and research institutes, these research centers also use the data to develop indicators and study the structure and development of science. These centers have been the primary drivers of innovation and critique in measuring research, as they have access to the full spectrum of bibliometric data. However, this creates an inequality in the field, in which research is concentrated among the few who can afford to buy and process these data. Furthermore, as the data are only licensed and not owned, they are always vulnerable to the shifting priorities of the company. For example, while the WoS continues to allow reuse by third-party licensees, Elsevier has limited such third-party reuse in favor of their own analytic products. Thus, applied bibliometric research projects with Scopus data are mostly performed through the research intelligence platform and services of Elsevier. Such barriers to access lead to decreased transparency of these datasets and, subsequently, reduce opportunities for measuring research.

It could be argued that market-driven products will lead to continuous competition and innovation in the system. The WoS held a monopoly for decades. Now many new products are arriving on the scene to challenge this monopoly, some from major companies (such as Microsoft, Google) and others from smaller research organizations (e.g., Semantic Scholar). These tools have the potential to lead to more inclusive datasets and lessen the barriers to entry for those who seek to measure research. However, the emergent tools presently suffer from issues of coverage and data quality. Therefore, the future of research measurement remains heavily dependent upon the continued success of a few corporations and their willingness to provide access to data.

What are the responsibilities of stakeholders?

Responsibility for appropriate research measurement is divided among several stakeholder groups, each with slightly different expertise and jurisdiction. In many ways, measuring research begins with the data. Data providers and indexers must be accountable for ensuring that their data are accurate and transparent, providing information on inclusion criteria and coverage. There is, however, no mechanism for holding data service providers accountable. Rather, the consumers of these data must be informed and use the data appropriately, given the known limitations. Users must remember that none of the data sources for measuring research are exhaustive. Therefore, indicators are, as their name suggests, indicative, but not demonstrative. For example, it is often assumed that coverage is comprehensive for basic production indicators. However, while the set of papers indexed by WoS may be appropriate for certain research questions, it is not appropriate to all research questions. What is provided by each of these databases is a population of indexed papers—neither a global nor representative sample. Users must understand the functional aspect of tools to be able to adequately interpret the data generated within these tools. For example, most platforms that provide bibliometric data were created for filtering or retrieval purposes. Using a retrieval tool as an evaluation tool has inherent limitations, as many of the criteria expected for evaluation (e.g., exhaustive coverage, standardization of data) may not be the same criteria as for a retrieval tool (e.g., high recall).

To respond to the need for institutional benchmarking, there has been a growth in corporations that buy or collect bibliometric data and provide analytic services for institutions. This has the danger of removing decision makers from the data used to make the decisions. Therefore, these corporations—such as Academic Analytics—have a responsibility to provide transparency in coverage as well as opportunities for individuals to access and, in the case of mistakes, mechanisms for redress. Furthermore, even when the data are clean, it may not accurately represent the state of the field, for example, collapsing disciplines (e.g., astronomy and physics) with fundamentally different publication and citation practices. The quality of output, therefore, varies dramatically by level of analysis and requires robust disambiguation. Without clean data and clear statements of limitations, reports from these tools may severely distort the realities of the system under measurement. Research administrators, who serve as the primary consumers of these tools, must be held responsible for the appropriate use of the data.

Policymakers play a critical role as both consumers of measurement and promoters of indicators. Metrics often serve as the basis of strategic decisions for both funding and policy. Policy, in turn, creates the incentive structures under which researchers operate. These policies are also tested through metrics. In general, research measurement should be used to help policymakers understand the system that they are attempting to govern and aid them in identifying appropriate interventions to achieve policy goals. Benchmarking and standardization are critically important for this stakeholder group. However, one should be cautious and acknowledge that the observed change could be due to the policy, not the actual fulfillment of the goals. For example, evaluations based on collaboration could lead to an increase in honorific authorship. In this context, the responsibility of policymakers is to make objectives and evaluation transparent.

Indicators are promoted by publishers and journal editors. Publishers often market their material on the basis of indicators, such as the JIF. As a result, this becomes the metric with which journals (and associated editors) are evaluated. This is a prime example of the abuse of an indicator, with adverse effects for the research community. The lack of field-normalization, the inappropriate citation window for most disciplines, and the lack of controls for skewness all suggest that the JIF is poorly developed even for the purpose it was intended to serve. However, even more problematic are the adverse sociological effects—the promotion and incentive structure around the indicators leads to alternations in both author and editor behavior. Editors play a central role as gatekeepers for scholarly communication. This honor comes with responsibility to ensure that they do not promote indicators that may be harmful to the scientific community. Furthermore, editors are in a prime position to advocate for the community with journal publishers, whose goals are often monetary rather than scientific.

The scientific community is the largest stakeholder group in research measurement. They are both the objects of study and the primary consumers of the data. It is essential that those who are being assessed are aware of and engaged in assessment exercises. When data are collected on individual researchers, these individuals should have access to data about themselves and rights of redress. At present, bibliometric data remain difficult to disambiguate at the individual level and are therefore highly error prone. Those who produce the scholarship are in the best position to evaluate the accuracy of their own records. Researchers must be vigilantly informed about the datasets that are being used to measure their work and maintain a dialogue with those who use these data to make decisions. It is often researchers themselves, as evaluators, who make these decisions; therefore, it is imperative that scholars are informed about the caveats for research data when performing evaluations.

Graduate students are not outside the bounds of this evaluation culture. In fact, the current generation of students may be more keenly aware of research indicators than any previous generation. It is the responsibility of educators, therefore, to ensure that these students are not raised to blindly seek metrics as an indicator of their own success. Students should be provided with training on appropriate construction and interpretation of metrics so that they do not propagate myths and misuse of metrics. It is acknowledged that hiring—particularly in academe—is a fiercely competitive space in which metrics are often used to discriminate among candidates. However, students should be trained first and foremost to focus on the inputs in the scientific system, not evaluations of outputs— that is, students should focus on the science first and not tailor their research program around indicators.

Although there are nuances to the responsibilities of each stakeholder group, there are five key issues that all stakeholder groups should keep in mind: (1) time, (2) data quality, (3) normalization, (4) coverage, and (5) alignment. In terms of time, publication and citation windows must be appropriate for the analysis. High-quality scholarship takes time to produce and citations take time to accumulate. Furthermore, rates of production and citation vary by discipline and have evolved over time. Studies that ignore the aspect of time are likely to lead to erroneous conclusions. Data quality can also lead to inaccurate results. Most bibliometric datasets have data quality issues, particularly when it comes to standard author or institution names. Careful cleaning must be done prior to analysis. Coverage and normalization are other critical issues: The data must have adequate coverage of the topic at hand and, if multiple disciplines are taken into account, must be normalized. The final issue of alignment is essential and informs the others. Bibliometric indicators should be compiled with a clear objective, and the selection of data must meet these criteria. Too often, studies are conducted where there is no alignment between the data, the indicators, and the research objective. Those in positions to evaluate and make decisions on the basis of these evaluations must ensure that the data and indicators are aligned with the overall goal of the evaluation.

Finally, it is the responsibility of the entire community to interpret the results with what Merton referred to as organized skepticism. Too often, quantitative results are given an aura of precision and authority that they do not always warrant. For example, the concept of statistical significance, which has for decades served as the cornerstone of quantitative research, has come under increased scrutiny. It is often both misapplied and misinterpreted. This is particularly the case in bibliometrics, where the concept of samples and populations are conflated. Appropriate sampling in addition to normal distributions are two assumptions that bibliometric data often violate. Bibliometric data, drawn from the WoS or Scopus, are essentially population-level data. However, it is a population of indexed articles and not a random sample of all papers that have been published. Furthermore, given the size of data in global research measurement exercises, there is a high probability of finding statistically significant results, even when no meaningfully valid difference exists. Therefore, in measuring research, as in all scientific work, the community has a responsibility to interpret results contextually.

What are the adverse effects of measurement?

Indicators incentivize behavior. In a value-neutral environment, measurements of output should have little impact upon the input. However, researchers, like all social creatures, are responsive to observation. As indicators are institutionalized in evaluative systems, researchers adapt their behavior to fit the measurement. Such adaptations have the potential to invert the scientific system, making the capital generated more important than the science itself. Goal displacement is a serious issue for research measurement in that it threatens to fundamentally distort the process it monitors (a phenomenon codified in 1976 by social psychologist Donald T. Campbell in a law that bears his name). In the words of Swiss economists Bruno Frey and Margit Osterloh, there is concern that research measurement has cultivated in scholars a "taste for rankings" over a "taste for science."

Science policy is often charged with moderating behaviors with explicit mandates or merely through the act of surveillance. A direct link between funding frameworks and production has been observed: When publication counts are prioritized, production increases; when high-impact work is weighted, publications in highly cited journals increases; when collaboration is promoted, there is an increase in collaborative work. This may demonstrate the efficacy of science policy. However, there are often unanticipated consequences. For example, when Australia adopted a new evaluation framework that rewarded publications in (then) ISI-indexed journals, they achieved the desired goal. However, while Australian research commanded a greater share of indexed works, the average impact of this work declined. Pressures on scientists to produce may yield greater production, but may lead to undesirable strategies—such as "salami slicing"—and lower quality work.

Citation-based formulae may also lead to negative effects. China, for example, provides monetary incentives to authors who publish in journals with a certain Impact Factor. This has been shown to dramatically increase the number of submissions to journals such as *Science*, but not lead to a corresponding increase in acceptances. As a result, the scientific community is burdened with reviewing work that was submitted to a journal that may not have been appropriate in topic or scope, but was prompted by a financial, rather than scientific, goal. The demands to achieve these goals have been linked to fraud and other abuses of the scientific system.

Even when the incentive is inherently positive, it might not be appropriate for all disciplines. For example, the increased emphasis on teamwork in educational settings, the growth of transnational corporations, and other globalization initiatives suggest that promoting collaboration is positive. Yet collaborative work may not be appropriate for every line of inquiry. Similarly, while promoting societal impact for research is laudable, it may prioritize applied over basic research, to the detriment of some fields. Therefore, science policy should be responsive to the diversity of science. Monolithic policies that fail to acknowledge the gross heterogeneity of the research landscape are most likely to lead to adverse effects.

The data and tools used to measure may also lead to adverse effects. Database coverage can lead to distortions in modes of production, with differential effects by discipline. For example, most bibliometric databases focus on journal articles. Indicators on the basis of these databases discriminate against those disciplines that produce in other formats. This may explain the increase of the use of journal articles—and corresponding relative decrease in the use of books—for disseminating new knowledge, particularly in the social sciences and humanities. Mode shifts affect the type of research produced: Journal articles are most suitable for smaller, more empirical work, and tend to favor timely quantitative work over more theoretical work. Furthermore, work can only be counted if it is indexed. Given the disparities in coverage by language, scholars are increasingly turning to producing in English, which may not be the most useful language for all domains of inquiry.

A critical flaw in measuring research is the misuse of indicators for levels of evaluation for which it was not intended. A distinction should be made between measurement of a scientific system (with data aggregated at the level of disciplines, institutions, and countries) and measurements of individuals. Bibliometrics is best applied at the system level to understand the structure and growth of basic research. Microlevel analyses are subject to significant errors: Issues of noncoverage and small mistakes can have large outcomes. As the law of large numbers would suggest, bibliometrics is more stable and valid at higher levels of aggregation. At the individual level, these data can be complementary, but should not replace other approaches to evaluation—there are simply too few observations and far too much variance to conclude meaningful information. The use of metrics at the individual level also stimulates a cyclicality in measurement; for example, there is a high correlation between those who are highly published, who are highly cited, and who command a large share of resources. The allocation of resources on the basis of highly correlated metrics can exacerbate the Matthew effect and create barriers for underrepresented populations to receive due rewards and resources.

It is clear that the research community has internalized research indicators. The audit culture in academe has given rise to fervor for counting and ranking. These metrics can yield important information for benchmarking and allocating resources. However, one must be wary of the false precision of research evaluation. The quantitative quality of metrics implies a certain truth value—yet there are no ground truths for concepts such as knowledge production or impact. Indicators that aim at measuring these concepts must be interpreted in light of their context and with known caveats of the data and tools. Absent this context, the indicators are, at best, meaningless and, at worst, dangerous. Along these lines, many prominent researchers have spoken out against metrics—disavowing the publications and publishers who promote certain metrics. However, it is a privilege of the elite to both create and reject indicators. Those who are well served by indicators generate cumulative advantage that propels them into the future. It is often those who are marginalized or are displaced by indicators who would benefit most from, but have the least opportunity to generate, new metrics. The inequalities created and perpetuated by indicators must be responsibly addressed by the scientific community.

What is the future of measuring research?

The Science Citation Index was a fairly outrageous endeavor in its time. Spend a few hours perusing the paper versions of the index and one wonders how Eugene Garfield envisioned a future for the service. However, advances in computational tools and the digital publishing of scholarly material have made new sources easier and old sources faster. The proliferation of tools is likely to continue, but with different audiences, permanence, and coverage. It is currently a consumer's market for indicators in which a metric exists for every conceivable dimension. Those advocating for new indicators often argue for them on the merits of inclusivity. However, multiplying indicators does not necessarily lead to increased equitability. For example, Nature Publishing Group created an index that ranks countries and institutions according to the number of papers they have published in Nature journals. This is a mechanism for generating capital—both economic and scientific—around a scholarly product. By creating an index (credible and desirable due to the academic capital of Nature), the publisher has incentivized publishing in its own journals, which generates significant economic capital. The reciprocity of economic and academic capital is an important element to consider in the evaluation of indicators. While biased rankings are easily dismissed when they are proposed by peripheral groups, publishers, institutions, and individuals with tremendous capital have greater persuasive abilities in the scholarly marketplace. This phenomenon is not relegated to the for-profit sector. For example, the National Institutes of Health in the United States—a leading funding agency for the biomedical sciences—created a new indicator (Relative Citation Ratio) to be used for internal evaluations and built the indicator into their web tool (iCite). The indicator has been heavily criticized by the bibliometric community, but it has remained relatively unchanged since it was proposed and has benefited from large exposure due to the brand association of the NIH. In short, capital generates capital, and the degree to which emerging tools are monetized or seen as public goods will certainly change the research landscape. Furthermore, while there are many benefits to the increased heterogeneity in metrics, this proliferation can lead to a "to each person, an indicator" scenario, in which indicators lose their ability to translate globally and communicate across disciplines.

The need for standards and interoperability has given rise to several initiatives that create crosswalks between datasets by the construction of unique identifiers. For instance, the Open Researcher Contributor Identification initiative—commonly known as ORCID—was incorporated in 2010 with the goal of providing a unique identifier for every researcher. ORCID facilitates author disambiguation by providing a unique identifier for researchers that can be associated with research products, regardless of genre or platform. By the end of 2016, ORCID had registered nearly 2.7 million accounts and hundreds of organizational members, including major research universities and publishing companies. A similar success story in standards can be found in Crossref, a digital object identifier registration agency launched in 2000 and run by Publishers International Linking Association Inc. (a not-for-profit association). The goal of Crossref is to facilitate the linking of documents across journals and platforms. It does not provide scientific content, but acts as a bridge—linking citations—between scientific content hosted on disparate sites. Crossref provides digital object identifiers (DOIs) for several document types, including preprints, journal articles, books, conference proceedings, dissertations, and datasets, for a total of 80 million DOIs assigned as of the end of 2016.

Tools have also been developed not only to link, but also to mine, scholarly documents. For example, the growing availability of full-text documents through self-archiving (i.e., green open access) has led to a few large-scale initiatives aimed at indexing and constructing indicators on the basis of these documents. For instance, Semantic Scholar, created by the Allen Institute for Artificial Intelligence, indices all papers in arXiv and DBLP—among other databases—which represents a large proportion of all published works in physics, mathematics, and computer science. Semantic Scholar provides document- and author-level citation indicators on the basis of this. Furthermore, it uses machine learning techniques to derive the relevance of a reference to a particular citing document.

However, as with Google Scholar, its bibliometric capabilities are limited to what is available through the platform. Furthermore, no automatic programming interface is available to mine and retrieve its content, so it remains unavailable for external evaluation. However, as open access is increasing, these initiatives are likely to gain traction, particularly given the potential for indicator construction on the basis of the context of citations.

The future of measuring research will rely heavily on tools that overlay on existing data, are interoperable across platforms, and can be modularized for specific needs. Researchers, administrators, and policymakers want data with increased coverage and tailored to their own preferences. This requires the availability of large-scale, heterogeneous datasets and the ability to quickly standardize, normalize, and contextualize these data. Many of the new users of these data are nonspecialists. Therefore, this requires tool developers and analysts to maintain a delicate balance in the provision of indicators. Simple indicators are easy to understand, but may be highly biased; complex indicators are often more precise, but also more difficult for a general audience to interpret. Furthermore, many of the new producers of metrics also lack a background in science studies and can unintentionally produce indicators that fail to meet basic standards of analysis—using inappropriate time windows, failing to adequately clean and disambiguate data, providing insufficient coverage, and failing to normalize. Such indicators can easily mislead and become divorced from the concept they purport to measure. The research community, therefore, must remain vigilant in monitoring emerging data and tools and in educating users on the appropriate application of indicators.

Experts in the field have long noted the complex web of political, economic, and scientific concerns in which the science system is embedded, but have argued for the ethical neutrality of metrics. However, it has become increasingly apparent that the way in which research is measured has dramatic effects on that which is being measured. Therefore, the use of various research indicators must first take into account these effects and ensure that indicators are not detrimental to the research community. Research evaluators would do well to heed the mantra of the medical profession: First do no harm. It is the responsibility of the scientific community to ensure that research is measured in a way that is productive and supports, rather than destroys, the scientific system it is set to observe. It is hoped that, by providing an accessible introduction to the historical underpinnings, the strengths and weaknesses of the data and indicators, and an interpretative lens, the present book is a step in this direction.

FURTHER READING

This book provides a synthesis of more than a century of work on the measurement of research. Due to the style of this series, we omitted explicit references from the chapters, but provide below full references to all the works that informed the writing of this book. To these we have added other key works that are useful for those seeking to acquire a basic understanding of measuring research. This list is by no means exhaustive—it is not meant to serve as a complete list of canonical works in the field. Rather, it is a way to both credit the works from which we drew insight and inspiration and also to serve as a resource for those seeking additional depth in this area of research and practice.

Chapter 1

Barabási, A. L., & Albert, R. (1999). Emergence of scaling in random networks. *Science, 286*(5439), 509–512.

Bourdieu, P. (1988). *Homo academicus*. Redwood City, CA: Stanford University Press.

Bourdieu, P. (2004). *Science of science and reflexivity*. Chicago: University of Chicago Press.

Cole, J., & Cole. S. (1973). *Social stratification in science*. Chicago: University of Chicago Press.

Cronin, B., & Sugimoto, C. R. (Eds.). (2014). *Beyond bibliometrics: Harnessing multidimensional indicators of scholarly impact*. Cambridge, MA: MIT Press.

De Bellis, N. (2009). *Bibliometrics and citation analysis: From the Science Citation Index to cybermetrics*. Lanham, MA: Scarecrow Press.

de Solla Price, D. J. (1963). *Little science, big science*. New York: Columbia University Press.

Elkana, Y., Lederberg, J., Merton, R. K., Thackray, A., & Zuckerman, H. (1978). *Towards a metric of science: The advent of science indicators.* New York: Wiley.

Gingras, Y. (2016). *Bibliometrics and research evaluation: Uses and abuses.* Cambridge, MA: MIT Press.

Godin, B. (2005). *Measurement and statistics on science and technology: 1920 to the Present.* London: Routledge.

Lazarsfeld, P. F., & Boudon, R. (1993). *On social research and its language.* Chicago, IL: University of Chicago Press.

Merton, R. K. (1968). The Matthew effect in science. *Science, 159*(3810), 56–63.

Merton, R. K. (1973). *The sociology of science: Theoretical and empirical investigations.* Chicago: University of Chicago Press.

Moed, H. F. (2004). *Citation analysis in research evaluation.* Dordrecht, NL: Springer.

Moed, H. F., Glänzel, W., & Schmoch U. (Eds.). (2005). *Handbook of quantitative science and technology research. The use of publication and patent statistics in studies of S&T systems.* Dordrech, NL: Kluwer Academic Publishers.

Rossiter, M. W. (1993). The Matthew Matilda effect in science. *Social Studies of Science, 23*(2), 325–341.

Small, H. G. (1978). Cited documents as concept symbols. *Social Studies of Science, 8*(3), 327–340.

Sugimoto, C. R. (Ed.). (2016). *Theories of informetrics and scholarly communication.* Berlin: De Gruyter Mouton.

Todeschini, R., & Baccini, A. (2016). *Handbook of bibliometric indicators: Quantitative tools for studying and evaluating research.* Weinheim: Wiley-VCH

van Raan, A. F. J. (1988). *Handbook of quantitative studies of science and technology.* Amsterdam: Elsevier.

Wouters, P. (1999). *The citation culture.* Doctoral Thesis, University of Amsterdam.

Chapter 2

Aguillo, I. (2012). Is Google Scholar useful for bibliometrics? A webometric analysis. *Scientometrics, 91*(2), 343–351.

Archambault, É., Campbell, D., Gingras, Y., & Larivière, V. (2009). Comparing bibliometric statistics obtained from the Web of Science and Scopus. *Journal of the Association for Information Science and Technology, 60*(7), 1320–1326.

Delgado López-Cózar, E., Robinson-García, N., & Torres-Salinas, D. (2014). The Google Scholar experiment: How to index false papers and manipulate bibliometric indicators. *Journal of the Association for Information Science and Technology, 65*(3), 446–454.

Elsevier. (2016). Scopus Content Coverage Guide. Available at: https://www.elsevier.com/__data/assets/pdf_file/0007/69451/scopus_content_coverage_guide.pdf

Garfield, E. (1955). Citation indexes for science. A new dimension in documentation through association of ideas. *Science, 122*(3159), 108–111.

Garfield, E. (1984). Genetics citation index: Experimental citation indexes to genetics with special emphasis on human genetics. *Essays of an Information Scientist, 7*, 515–522.

Garfield, E. (1990). How ISI selects journals for coverage: Quantitative and qualitative considerations. *Current Contents, 13*(22), 185–193.

Gordin, M. D. (2015). *Scientific Babel: How science was done before and after global English.* Chicago: University of Chicago Press.

Jacsó, P. (2011). Google Scholar duped and deduped—the aura of "robometrics." *Online Information Review, 35*(1), 154–160.

Kawashima, H., & Tomizawa, H. (2015). Accuracy evaluation of Scopus Author ID based on the largest funding database in Japan. *Scientometrics, 103*(3), 1061–1071.

Labbé, C. (2010). Ike Antkare one of the great stars in the scientific firmament. *ISSI Newsletter 6*(2), 48–52.

Mongeon, P., & Paul-Hus, A. (2016). The journal coverage of Web of Science and Scopus: A comparative analysis. *Scientometrics, 106*(1), 213–228.

Orduna-Malea, E., Ayllón, J. M., Martín-Martín, A., & López-Cózar, E. D. (2015). Methods for estimating the size of Google Scholar. *Scientometrics, 104*(3), 931–949.

Robinson-García, N., Jiménez-Contreras, E., & Torres-Salinas, D. (2015). Analyzing data citation practices using the data citation index. *Journal of the Association for Information Science and Technology, 67*(12), 2964–2975.

Sugimoto, C. R., & Weingart, S. (2015). The kaleidoscope of disciplinarity. *Journal of Documentation, 71*(4), 775–794.

Testa, J. (2016). The Thomson Reuters journal selection process. Available at: http://wokinfo.com/essays/journal-selection-process/?utm_source=false&utm_medium=false&utm_campaign=false

Torres-Salinas, D., Rodríguez-Sánchez, R., Robinson-García, N., Fdez-Valdivia, J., & García, J. A. (2013). Mapping citation patterns of book chapters in the Book Citation Index. *Journal of Informetrics, 7*(2), 412–424.

Chapter 3

Acharya, A., Verstak, A., Suzuki, H., Henderson, S., Iakhiaev, M., Lin, C. C. Y., & Shetty, N. (2014). Rise of the rest: The growing impact of non-elite journals. arXiv preprint, arXiv:1410.2217.

Archambault, É., & Larivière V. (2009). History of journal impact factor: Contingencies and consequences. *Scientometrics, 79*(3), 639–653.

Bergstrom, C. T., & West, J. D. (2016). Comparing impact factor and Scopus CiteScore. Available at: http://eigenfactor.org/projects/posts/citescore.php

Bergstrom, C. T., West, J. D., & Wiseman, M. A. (2008). The Eigenfactor™ metrics. *Journal of Neuroscience, 28*(45), 11433–11434.

Bertin, M., Atanassova, I., Sugimoto, C. R., & Lariviere, V. (2016). The linguistic patterns and rhetorical structure of citation context: An approach using n-grams. *Scientometrics, 109*(3), 1417–1434.

Birnholtz, J. P. (2006). What does it mean to be an author? The intersection of credit, contribution, and collaboration in science. *Journal of the American Society for Information Science and Technology, 57*(13), 1758–1770.

Bollen, J., Van de Sompel, H., Hagberg, A., & Chute, R. (2009). A principal component analysis of 39 scientific impact measures. *PLoS ONE, 4*(6), e6022.

Bornmann, L. (2011). Scientific peer review. *Annual Review of Information Science and Technology, 45*(1), 197–245.

Bornmann, L., & Daniel, H. D. (2008). What do citation counts measure? A review of studies on citing behavior. *Journal of Documentation, 64*(1), 45–80.

Catalini, C., Lacetera, N., & Oettl, A. (2015). The incidence and role of negative citations in science. *Proceedings of the National Academy of Sciences, 112*(45), 13823–13826.

Cole, S., & Cole, J. R. (1967). Scientific output and recognition: A study in the operation of the reward system in science. *American Sociological Review, 32*(3), 377–390.

Galison, P., & Biagioli, M. (Eds.). (2003). *Scientific authorship: Credit and intellectual property in science.* New York: Routledge.

Garfield, E. (1979). Is citation analysis a legitimate evaluation tool? *Scientometrics, 1*(4), 359–375.

Gauffriau, M., & Larsen, P. O. (2005). Counting methods are decisive for rankings based on publication and citation studies. *Scientometrics, 64*(1), 85–93.

Glänzel, W., & Moed, H. F. (2002). Journal impact measures in bibliometric research. *Scientometrics, 53*(2), 171–193.

Glänzel, W., & Schoepflin, U. (1995). A bibliometric study on ageing and reception processes of scientific literature. *Journal of Information Science, 21*, 37–54.

González-Pereira, B., Guerrero-Bote, V. P., & Moya-Anegón, F. (2010). A new approach to the metric of journals' scientific prestige: The SJR indicator. *Journal of Informetrics, 4*(3), 379–391.

Griliches, Z. (Ed.). (2007). *R&D, patents and productivity.* Chicago: University of Chicago Press.

Grossetti, M., Eckert, D., Gingras, Y., Jégou, L., Larivière, V., & Milard, B. (2014). Cities and the geographical deconcentration of scientific activity: A multilevel analysis of publications (1987–2007). *Urban Studies, 51*(10), 2219–2234.

Hagen, N. T. (2010). Harmonic publication and citation counting: Sharing authorship credit equitably—not equally, geometrically or arithmetically. *Scientometrics, 84*(3), 785–793.

Hamilton, D. P. (1990). Publishing by—and for?—the numbers. *Science, 250*(4986), 1331–1332.

Hirsch, J. E. (2005). An index to quantify an individual's scientific research output. *Proceedings of the National Academy of Sciences of the United States of America, 102*(46), 16569–16572.

ICMJE. (2016). Recommendations. http://www.icmje.org/recommendations/

Jaffe, A. B., & Trajtenberg, M. (2002). *Patents, citations, and innovations: A window on the knowledge economy.* Cambridge, MA: MIT Press.

Katz, J. S., & Martin, B. R. (1997). What is research collaboration? *Research Policy, 26*(1), 1–18.

Larivière, V., Archambault, É., Gingras, Y. (2008). Long-term variations in the aging of scientific literature: From exponential growth to steady-state science (1900–2004). *Journal of the American Society for Information Science and Technology, 59*(2), 288–296.

Larivière, V., Desrochers, N., Macaluso, B., Mongeon, P., Paul-Hus, A., & Sugimoto, C. R. (2016). Contributorship and division of labor in knowledge production. *Social Studies of Science, 46*(3), 417–435.

Larivière, V., Gingras, Y., & Archambault, É. (2009). The decline in the concentration of citations, 1900–2007. *Journal of the American Society for Information Science and Technology, 60*(4), 858–862.

Lariviere, V., Kiermer, V., MacCallum, C. J., McNutt, M., Patterson, M., Pulverer, B., Swaminathan, S., Taylor, S., & Curry, S. (2016). A simple proposal for the publication of journal citation distributions. *Biorxiv,* 062109.

Larivière, V., Lozano, G. A., & Gingras, Y. (2014). Are elite journals declining? *Journal of the Association for Information Science and Technology, 65*(4), 649–655.

Lee, C. J., Sugimoto, C. R., Zhang, G., & Cronin, B. (2013). Bias in peer review. *Journal of the American Society for Information Science and Technology, 64*(1), 2–17.

Leydesdorff, L., Bornmann, L., Mutz, R., & Opthof, T. (2011). Turning the tables on citation analysis one more time: Principles for comparing sets of documents. *Journal of the American Society for Information Science and Technology, 62*(7), 1370–1381.

Li, D., & Agha, L. (2015). Big names or big ideas: Do peer-review panels select the best science proposals? *Science, 348*(6233), 434–438.

Lozano, G. A., Larivière, V., & Gingras, Y. (2012). The weakening relationship between the Impact Factor and papers' citations in the digital age. *Journal of the American Society for Information Science and Technology, 63*(11), 2140–2145.

McCain, K. W. (2014). Obliteration by incorporation. In B. Cronin & C. R. Sugimoto (Eds.), *Beyond bibliometrics: Harnessing multidimensional indicators of scholarly impact* (pp. 129–149). Cambridge, MA: MIT Press.

Moed, H. F. (2010). Measuring contextual citation impact of scientific journals. *Journal of Informetrics, 4*(3), 265–277.

Moed, H. F., & Van Leeuwen, T.N. (1995). Improving the accuracy of Institute for Scientific Information's journal impact factors. *Journal of American Society of Information Science, 46*, 461–467.

Moravcsik, M. J., & Murugesan P. (1975). Some results on the function and quality of citations. *Social Studies of Science, 5*(1), 86–92.

OECD. (2015). *Frascati manual 2015: Guidelines for collecting and reporting data on research and experimental development, the measurement of scientific, technological and innovation activities.* Paris: OECD Publishing.

Paul-Hus, A., Mongeon, P., Sainte-Marie, M., & Larivière, V. (2017). The sum of it all: Revealing collaboration patterns by combining authorship and acknowledgements. *Journal of Informetrics, 11*(1), 80–87.

Pontille, D. (2003). Authorship practices and institutional contexts in sociology: Elements for a comparison of the United States and France. *Science, Technology & Human Values, 28*(2), 217–243.

Priem, J. (2014). Altmetrics. In B. Cronin & C. R. Sugimoto (Eds.), *Beyond bibliometrics: Harnessing multi-dimensional indicators of performance* (pp. 263–287). Cambridge, MA: MIT Press.

Rousseau, R., García-Zorita, C., & Sanz-Casado, E. (2013). The h-bubble. *Journal of Informetrics, 7*(2), 294–300.

Seglen, P. O. (1992). The skewness of science. *Journal of the American Society for Information Science, 43*(9), 628–638.

Shapin, S. (1989). The invisible technician. *American Scientist, 77*(6), 554–563.

Small, H. (1973). Co-citation in the scientific literature: A new measure of the relationship between two documents. *Journal of the Association for Information Science and Technology, 24*(4), 265–269.

Sugimoto, C. R. (2016). "Attention is not impact" and other challenges for altmetrics. Wiley Exchanges Blog. June 24, 2015. https://hub.wiley.com/community/exchanges/discover/blog/2015/06/23/attention-is-not-impact-and-other-challenges-for-altmetrics

Sugimoto, C. R., Work, S., Larivière, V., & Haustein, S. (2016). Scholarly use of social media and altmetrics: A review of the literature. arXiv:1608.08112.

Van Leeuwen, T. (2008). Testing the validity of the Hirsch-index for research assessment purposes. *Research Evaluation, 17*(2), 157.

Verstak, A., Acharya, A., Suzuki, H., Henderson, S., Iakhiaev, M., Lin, C. C. Y., & Shetty, N. (2014). On the shoulders of giants: The growing impact of older articles. arXiv preprint arXiv:1411.0275.

Wagner, C. S., Roessner, J. D., Bobb, K., Klein, J. T., Boyack, K. W., Keyton, J., Rafols, I., & Börner, K. (2011). Approaches to understanding and measuring interdisciplinary scientific research (IDR): A review of the literature. *Journal of Informetrics, 5*(1), 14–26.

Wallace, M. L., Larivière, V., & Gingras, Y. (2009). Modeling a century of citation distributions. *Journal of Informetrics, 3*(4), 296–303.

Waltman, L., Calero-Medina, C., Kosten, J., Noyons, E. C. M., Tijssen, R. J. W., Van Eck, N. J., Van Leeuwen, T. N., Van Raan, A .F. J., Visser, M. S., & Wouters, P. (2012). The Leiden Ranking 2011/2012: Data collection, indicators, and interpretation. *Journal of the American*

Society for Information Science and Technology, 63(12), 2419–2432. arXiv:1202.3941.

Waltman, L., & Van Eck, N. J. (2012). The inconsistency of the h-index. *Journal of the American Society for Information Science and Technology, 63*(2), 406–415.

Waltman, L., Van Eck, N. J., Van Leeuwen, T. N., Visser, M. S., & Van Raan, A. F. J. (2011a). Towards a new crown indicator: An empirical analysis. *Scientometrics, 87*(3), 467–481.

Waltman, L., Van Eck, N. J., Van Leeuwen, T. N., Visser, M. S., & Van Raan, A. F. J. (2011b). Towards a new crown indicator: Some theoretical considerations. *Journal of Informetrics, 5*(1), 37–47.

Wilsdon, J., Allen, L., Belfiore, E., Campbell, P., Curry, S., Hill, S., Jones, R., Kain, R., Kerridge, S., Thelwall, M., Tinkler, J., Viney, I., Wouters, P., Hill, J., & Johnson, B. (2015). *The metric tide: Report of the independent review of the role of metrics in research assessment and management.* London: SAGE.

Wouters, P., & Costas, R. (2012). *Users, narcissism and control–tracking the impact of scholarly publications in the 21st century.* Utrecht, NL: SURF Foundation.

Chapter 4

Butler, L. (2003). Explaining Australia's increased share of ISI publications—The effects of a funding formula based on publication counts. *Research Policy, 32*(1), 143–155.

Hicks, D., Wouters, P., Waltman, L., De Rijcke, S., & Rafols, I. (2015). The Leiden Manifesto for research metrics. *Nature, 520*(7548), 429.

Larivière, V., Haustein, S, & Mongeon, P. (2015). The oligopoly of academic publishers in the digital era. *PLoS ONE, 10*(6), e0127502.

Osterloh, M., & Frey, B. S. (2015). Ranking games. *Evaluation Review, 39*(1), 102–129.

Schneider, J. W. (2013). Caveats for using statistical significance tests in research assessments. *Journal of Informetrics, 7*(1), 50–62.

Stephan, P. (2012). Research efficiency: Perverse incentives. *Nature, 484*(7392), 29–31.

Welpe, I. M., Wollersheim, J., Ringelhan, S., & Osterloh, M. (Eds.). (2015). *Incentives and performance: Governance of knowledge-intensive organizations.* Cham, CH: Springer International Publishing.

Wouters, P., Glänzel, W., Gläser, J., & Rafols, I. (2013). The dilemmas of performance indicators of individual researchers—An urgent debate in bibliometrics. *ISSI Newsletter, 9*(3), 48–53.

INDEX